So you really want t

LATIN
PREP

BOOK 1

Answer Book

NEW EDITION OF LATIN PREP 1 PUPIL'S BOOK

As explained in the preface to the new edition of Latin Prep 1 (ISBN-13: 978 1 902984 98 8), the new edition contains exercises not previously published.

To obtain the answers to these new exercises you can either download a PDF from the title page for the Answer Book on our website www.galorepark.co.uk or send a stamped self-addressed envelope to the address below to obtain a printed sheet (please mark your correspondence Latin Prep 1 Additional Answers).

Galore Park Publishing, 19/21 Sayers Lane, Tenterden, Kent TN30 6BW

So you really want to learn

LATIN PREP

BOOK 1
Answer Book

Theo Zinn M.A. (Oxon.)

Series Editor: Nicholas Oulton M.A. (Oxon.)

GALORE PARK

Published by Galore Park Publishing Ltd.,
PO Box 96, Cranbrook TN17 4WS
www.galorepark.co.uk

Cover design by GKA Design, London WC2
Printed by Thanet Press Ltd

ISBN 1 902984 16 1

First published 2004

Also available:
Pupil's book   1902984153

Acknowledgements

My special thanks are due as ever to Nick Oulton for his unfailing courtesy and encouragement and his many creative suggestions, thanks to which I hope this book will prove useful. I might have added 'without which it would have been written in half the time', but I have an uncomfortable feeling that this would have been too obviously cribbed from the dedication by P.G. Wodehouse of that great work 'The Heart of a Goof'.

As ever, again, I am grateful to Peter Brown of Trinity College, Oxford, who has given so much of his time without complaint to helping me sort out whole arrays of ticklish problems, bringing sense and sanity to all of them without ever making me feel stupid or ignorant!

I thank also Peter and Jackie Fennymore for their never-failing support and encouragement which has been so immensely valuable.

And I am grateful to Rupert Fennymore for continuing to place his outstanding IT skills at our disposal.

Finally all mistakes and inadequacies in this book are my fault and my fault only.

Author's preface

The main purpose of this book is to give suggested answers to all the exercises contained in Latin Prep Book 1. I must admit that this has proved rather more difficult a task than I had anticipated it would be. This is chiefly because so often there is more than one correct answer to many a question. I have not always given every possible answer, but I have often given an alternative, particularly when we are dealing with the so-called 'perfect tense', hoping to make pupils fully aware from the word go that this tense can have two such different meanings.

For those who feel that my dissertation on translating the 'imperfect' goes a bit (or a lot!) over the top, there is an obvious solution. Skip it, or a least skip part of it. I wouldn't say quite the same about my extensive piece on quantities and stress, since if pupils are to be encouraged to read aloud, it is important that they should do this correctly from the start. Of course those teachers who know it all will skip this section. But I feel that there may be some who are not so deeply involved in it as I have become over many years of preparing pupils for the Reading Competitions fostered in so many places by the Classical Association, which are such a splendid feature of a Classical education. This, as you may guess, is one of the bees in my bonnet.

Finally, if I do not always adopt the most learned approach to every subject, it is chiefly because my main concern, for the moment, is to make Latin as cheerfully approachable as possible.

TLZ

Contents

Chapter 1 1
General points 1
On translating English into Latin 1
On word order 1
A general note on translating sentences 1
Salvē! 2
On translating the present tense 3
On vocabulary learning 4
On the verb *dō* 4
Chapter 2 5
On proper nouns 5
On the names of the cases 5
On neatness 5
On marking exercises, including stories 5
On *habitō* 5
On *cavē* 6
On stories 7
On subjects and objects 8
Chapter 3 12
On names 12
On quantities 12
Chapter 4 18
On *ā/ab* = by 18
On the imperfect and past tenses 18
On *Graecus* = a Greek man 23
Chapter 5 24
On the perfect tense 24
On the imperfect and past tenses (again) 24
On *in* + accusative 24
Chapter 6 29
On *respondeō* 29
On questions 29
On easier English into Latin sentences 29

Chapter 7 35

On the 4th conjugation 35

On *vēnī, vīdī, vīcī!* 37

Chapter 8 39

On adverbs 39

Chapter 9 45

On subordinate clauses and word order (the Chinese puzzle) 45

Chapter 10 49

On *nunc est bibendum* 49

On stories etc. 49

Hints on doing exams 49

Chapter 1

General points

We shall begin each chapter with some general remarks about the material to be covered and some points which may arise. These are in no way meant to be exhaustive. Teachers (or those helping the pupils at home) will have to decide how much attention to pay to these extra little 'words of wisdom' (?) and when (if ever) to introduce them.

On translating English into Latin

I should perhaps begin by explaining why there are so many exercises in this book that require translation from English into Latin. There are basically two reasons for this. The first is that I regard them as the best possible training for translating Latin into English. The second is that they will form an incomparable basis for handling the more difficult syllabuses that follow. These sentences are used for reinforcing the various teaching points and regularly stray beyond the narrow confines of the Level 1 syllabus for "language manipulation". However, from Chapter 6 onwards I have always included some sentences which stick rigidly to the Level 1 syllabus, i.e. those which require no more than a knowledge of the 1st and 2nd declensions (nominative and accusative singular only) and the 1st and 2nd conjugations (present tense only).

On word order

The strongest place in a Latin sentence is at the end, and as the verb is the strongest part of speech (you can hardly have a sentence without one) it tends to come at the end, binding the whole sentence together, as it were. Any other part of speech coming at the end of a Latin sentence or clause would therefore be stressed, because it would not be expected to be there. In Terence's *Phormio*, the old man Demipho has been asking three friends of his for legal advice. They ask if he requires their services any longer. In fact they have completely muddled him up. However he replies with consummate politeness '*fēcistis probē*', 'you have done splendidly', thus putting wonderfully dredged up stress on the adverb *probē*. Adverbs are on the whole rather weak parts of speech.

However, we can see already on page 8 that in some *questions* the verb (for no obvious reason) does not come at the end of the sentence. One can allow a lot of freedom on this.

On pp 8-9 and on p 11 genders and the adjective *Rōmānus* are thrown around, to give us the flavour of things; but we soon become duly methodical!

A general note on translating sentences

Over and over again we shall find that there is more than one correct way of translating a sentence, especially from Latin into English. I often give a number of possibilities, but I do not claim that these are exhaustive, and I should not like to think of a pupil's being marked down, if he or she comes up with a possible version which I have not mentioned. This is obviously the case with 'a' or 'the'. Of course in Exercise 1.8, where all three forms of the present tense are specifically asked for, they should be given.

Salvē!

Salvē is the singular imperative of the verb *salveō* (= "to be well"; hence "greetings" or "hello"), a form the pupils will not meet for some time to come. At this stage, when they know nothing at all, this should not concern us (or them!).

Sulpicia is a woman. Aulus is a farmer.
[In speech bubble:] "I am Sulpicia. I am a woman."
[In speech bubble:] "I am Aulus. I am a farmer."
"Hello, Sulpicia. Where is Marcus?"
"Marcus is here. Cassia is also here. Cassia is a girl."
[In speech bubble:] "I am Quintus. I am a poet."
"Who is Quintus?"
"Quintus is a poet."
"Cassia, where are Aulus and Sulpicia?"
"Aulus and Sulpicia are here."
Claudia and Cassia are girls. They are Roman girls.
"Hello. We are girls."
Laelia is also a Roman girl.
"Hello. I am a Roman girl."
Gnaeus is Roman. Sextus is Roman.
Gnaeus and Sextus are not farmers. They are sailors.
"Hello. We are sailors."

Note that the pronoun *ego* is regularly mispronounced by beginners. The '*o*' is unashamedly short. The trisyllabic *poēta* also causes a few problems: *po-ē-ta* (see Pupil's Book, page 6).

Exercise 1.1

1. *īnsulae*
2. *poētae*
3. *nautae*
4. *sagittae*
5. *hastae*

Exercise 1.2

1. Who is here?
2. Aulus is here.
3. The poet and the farmer are here.
4. Sulpicia and Laelia are Roman.
5. Quintus and Aulus are here.
6. Where is the Roman woman?
7. A Roman girl and a Roman farmer are here.
8. I am Sulpicia, you are Laelia.
9. We are sailors.
10. You are farmers.

Exercise 1.3

1. *tū puella es, sed ego fēmina sum.*
2. *nōs agricolae sumus, sed vōs nautae estis.*
3. *tū Quīntus es.*
4. *vōs puellae estis.*
5. *tū Sulpicia es, sed ego Laelia sum.*

Exercise 1.4

1.	*Britannia*	4.	*Ītalia*
2.	*Gallia*	5.	*Hispānia*
3.	*Germānia*	6.	*Hibernia*

Exercise 1.5

Pupils should be encouraged to see the connexions between English and Latin words from an early stage. They usually enjoy this and it provides an invaluable aid to learning vocabulary. I should at this stage state that my spelling of 'connexion' is rooted in my Classical education. The word is derived from the Latin verb *connectō*, with supine *connexum*.

1.	aquarium	5.	nautical
2.	feminine	6.	patriotic
3.	poet	7.	insular
4.	agriculture	8.	egoist

Exercise 1.6

For example, any four verbs laid out as follows:

aedificō, aedificās, aedificat, aedificāmus, aedificātis, aedificant = I build

ambulō, ambulās, ambulat, ambulāmus, ambulātis, ambulant = I walk

clāmō, clāmās, clāmat, clāmāmus, clāmātis, clāmant = I shout

rogō, rogās, rogat, rogāmus, rogātis, rogant = I ask, ask for

Exercise 1.7

1. *aedificō, aedificās, aedificat, aedificāmus, aedificātis, aedificant*
2. *ambulō, ambulās, ambulat, ambulāmus, ambulātis, ambulant*
3. *habitō, habitās, habitat, habitāmus, habitātis, habitant*
4. *festīnō, festīnās, festīnat, festīnāmus, festīnātis, festīnant*
5. *clāmō, clāmās, clāmat, clāmāmus, clāmātis, clāmant*

On translating the present tense

The problem here, as so often, lies with the English. If the verb expresses an act, the regular present tense is 'I am + present participle.'

E.g.   'What are you doing?'
        'I am calling the slave.'

But if it expresses a state or condition, the present tense is regularly the simple verb, e.g. 'I know,' 'I love' etc. Again, the simple form is used when a verb expresses frequency or habit, e.g. 'he works every day' or 'she plays the piano.' The 'do' form is used in questions and negatives and for stress. This is not meant to be an English lesson; our problem arises when we are asked to translate *puellam amō* into English. 'I am loving the girl' is bad English, and 'I love the girl' would be right. But with *Gāium vocō*, 'I am calling Gaius' would be right while 'I call Gaius' would in most cases be wrong.

Perhaps this could be gently and gradually imparted to one's pupils, and I certainly would not treat 'I am loving' or 'I call' in these two examples as wrong for a long, long time.

Exercise 1.8

1. We call, are calling, do call.
2. You (pl.) inhabit, are inhabiting, do inhabit.
3. They love, are loving, do love.
4. You (s.) walk, are walking, do walk.
5. I build, am building, do build.
6. He, she or it shouts, is shouting, does shout.
7. You (pl.) work, are working, do work.
8. They kill, are killing, do kill.
9. You (s.) hurry, are hurrying, do hurry.
10. We sing, are singing, do sing.

Exercise 1.9

1. *festīnat*
2. *cantant*
3. *ambulās*
4. *Aulus nōn cantat*
5. *Sulpicia labōrat*
6. *agricola clāmat*
7. *rogō*
8. *necant*
9. *vocāmus*
10. *nōn festīnant*

On vocabulary learning

Regular learning and revision of vocabulary is an important part of learning a language. Pupils grow in confidence when they find that they know the words, even if the task of translating them correctly proves a little harder than they might think. Conversely, how many times do we hear pupils crying 'But I didn't know any of the words'!

On the verb dō

The short '*a*'s in this verb are a joy that some pupils will delight in, allowing them to show off their knowledge of the fact that such '*a*'s are generally long in this conjugation. The '*a*' is only long in the following forms: *dās* (2nd singular, present indicative), *dā* (2nd singular, imperative); *dāns* (present participle; long before -*ns*).

Chapter 2

On proper nouns

Pupils need to be aware from the start that proper nouns (i.e. names) must always be translated into the nominative singular (or nominative plural if they don't have a nominative singular). E.g. *videō Quīntum* = 'I see Quintus', *Coriolōs cēpit* = 'he took Corioli' (a town in Latium, not far from Rome). It is a frequent tendency to rename Quintus "Quintum", simply because in a Latin piece his name has appeared in the accusative case.

Some names are so well-known that they are regularly referred to in their Anglicised forms (e.g. Rome rather than Roma, Athens rather than Athenae, etc.).

On the names of the cases

Perhaps I should have said that 'nominative' comes from *nōmen* name. But this tells us nothing about its use; nor does the fact that the word 'noun' itself comes from *nōmen* help very much. 'Accusative' seems to me a nasty, suspicious name, though I could perhaps have slipped in the verb *accūsō*, which is conveniently 1st conjugation. 'Genitive' is a bit too biological perhaps, and 'Ablative' only expresses the 'from' meaning of this case; besides the verb *auferō* from which it comes is so grossly irregular that I feel it should not be mentioned at this stage, even in hushed whispers. This leaves us with the 'Vocative' and 'Dative' – the only sensibly named cases. Perhaps I should have said that they are derived from *vocō* and *dō*, and perhaps answers to questions about the other cases can be gently postponed.

On neatness

As I've admitted in the Pupil's Book (page 17), I find it very much against my nature to be neat. In my University days I faithfully filled note-books with lecture notes. But they were so illegible and so uninvitingly set down by me that I could hardly read a word of them. This sad story of mine could perhaps drive it home to the pupils that with all this fuss about neatness we have their best interests at heart.

On marking exercises, including stories

Whereas I have generally given more than one version of a sentence or an answer (in the case of the stories), I hope pupils will not be marked down for not doing this, unless it is specifically asked for. I know only too well that there is not always one correct answer and that in spite of all the praise heaped upon the Latin language for its accuracy, it can often be ambiguous. I will say a little more about this later, with special reference to tenses.

On habitō

I'm worried about the frequent translation of *habitō* as 'I live', unless it is made abundantly clear that it never means 'I am alive'. I prefer to teach that *habitō* means 'I inhabit' (transitive) or 'I dwell' (intransitive) which, if nothing else, expands their English vocabulary a little.

On cavē

Perhaps wrongly I haven't explained *cavē*, which I now think may not be as familiar as I thought it was. It is the imperative of *caveō* = 'I am wary'. In the past, if boys were fooling about and one of them saw the master coming, he would shout '*cavē!*' ('beware!'), using the old English pronunciation (kay-vee). Apologies to those who know all this.

caveō, cavēre, cāvī, cautum can also be transitive, as in *cavē canem* = 'Beware of the dog'.

Exercise 2.1

1. Farmer is a concrete noun.
2. Poet is a concrete noun.
3. Angry is not a noun.
4. Freedom is an abstract noun.
5. Free is not a noun.
6. Hippopotamus is a concrete noun.
7. Anxiety is an abstract noun.
8. Teacher is a concrete noun.
9. Teachers are concrete nouns.
10. Teaches is not a noun.

Exercise 2.2

1.

	Singular	Plural
Nominative	*fēmina*	*fēminae*
Vocative	*fēmina*	*fēminae*
Accusative	*fēminam*	*fēminās*
Genitive	*fēminae*	*fēminārum*
Dative	*fēminae*	*fēminīs*
Ablative	*fēminā*	*fēminīs*

2.

	Singular	Plural
Nominative	*agricola*	*agricolae*
Vocative	*agricola*	*agricolae*
Accusative	*agricolam*	*agricolās*
Genitive	*agricolae*	*agricolārum*
Dative	*agricolae*	*agricolīs*
Ablative	*agricolā*	*agricolīs*

3.

	Singular	Plural
Nominative	*hasta*	*hastae*
Vocative	*hasta*	*hastae*
Accusative	*hastam*	*hastās*
Genitive	*hastae*	*hastārum*
Dative	*hastae*	*hastīs*
Ablative	*hastā*	*hastīs*

This sort of exercise is immensely valuable for teaching pupils how nouns of the same declension form a set pattern. If they get mutinous, or if their handwriting is as poor as mine, a simple exercise to bring in a bit of IT is to get them to type out *puella* as set out in the Pupil's Book on page 17. Then ask them to do an 'Edit, search and replace'. Searching for *puell* and replacing it with *fēmin* allows them to set out the noun *fēmina* in full with a few simple key strokes. As well as being quick and efficient, it teaches them which part of the word is changing and which part is remaining the same. They can then have fun doing this process with any number of 1st declension nouns and plastering the walls with beautifully laid out Latin nouns. N.B. I owe this paragraph entirely to Nicholas Oulton!

Exercise 2.3

1.	The <u>dog</u> is barking.
2.	The <u>girls</u> are singing.
3.	<u>Sulpicia</u> and <u>Aulus</u> are singing.
4.	<u>Laelia</u> is a woman.
5.	<u>Aulus</u> is a farmer.

Exercise 2.4

1.	*poēta*
2.	*puella*
3.	*puellae*
4.	*Sulpicia (et) Cassia*
5.	*agricolae*

On stories

Perhaps our stories are not quite literary masterpieces. To some extent this is due to the syllabus. We cannot, for example, use the pronouns 'he', 'she', 'it' or 'they', which is rather inhibiting and leads to inevitable repetition of proper names. Another rather grim restriction is imposed on the author by a complete embargo on the future tense; this has led, I fear, to some rather clumsy paraphrases. I have allowed myself some extra words shown on the right-hand side of the stories, and have persuaded myself that they will come in useful one day.

Some of these stories I have made up; others I have taken from mythology. Little did I realise, in my innocence, how many different versions there could be of the latter. I only hope that I have generally ended up with something reasonably familiar. Please do not take such requirements as 'Translate the passage into <u>beautiful</u> English prose' (see Pupil's Book, top of page 29) too seriously. Similar expressions occur throughout!

Exercise 2.5

1.	Cassia is a girl; Aulus is a farmer. Cassia is singing and Aulus is shouting. "Why are you shouting?" asks Cassia. Sulpicia is a woman. Quintus is a poet. Sulpicia and Quintus are singing. "Why are you singing?" ask Claudia and Aulus. "Where are we?" asks Laelia. "Here is land, here are waves; it is an island", shouts Lucius.

	Gnaeus and Sextus are sailors. Lucius and Marcus are farmers. The sailors and the farmers are fighting. The girls and the women are not fighting. The queen calls and the maid-servants hurry. "Why are the farmers and the sailors fighting?" asks the queen. "They are sailors; they are farmers," the maid-servants shout. "Sailors and farmers always fight." It is an island!

2.	(a) Nominative.
	(b) Because it is governed by two subjects, Sulpicia and Quintus.
	(c) They are fighting.
	(d) They hurry.
	(e) Because sailors and farmers always fight.

Exercise 2.6

1. <u>Cassia</u>, where are you?
2. <u>Laelia</u>, why are you crying?
3. <u>Laelia</u> and <u>Marcus</u>, why are you shouting?
4. Marcus is singing, <u>Sulpicia</u>.
5. Hello, <u>girls</u>.

Exercise 2.7

1. *Sulpicia*
2. *puellae*
3. *Cassia*
4. *Laelia et Cassia*
5. *agricolae*

On subjects and objects

It would be hard to overstate the importance of this lesson. If pupils can grasp from the beginning that it is the *form* of the words, not their *order*, which tells us who is doing what to whom, then the world will be a better and safer place.

Exercise 2.8

	S	V	O
1.	The woman	loves	the daughter.
2.	The farmer	watches	the girls.
3.	The girl	calls	the farmer.
4.	The poet	loves	the goddess.
5.	The farmer	kills	the maid-servant.

Exercise 2.9

1. The woman is nominative; the daughter is accusative.
2. The farmer is nominative; the girls are accusative.
3. The girl is nominative; the farmer is accusative.
4. The poet is nominative; the goddess is accusative.
5. The farmer is nominative; the maid-servant is accusative.

Exercise 2.10

1. *amō* is transitive.
2. *festīnō* is intransitive.
3. *aedificō* is transitive.
4. *labōrō* is intransitive.
5. *laudō* is transitive.

Exercise 2.11

	S	O	V	
1.	*puella*	*nautam*	*vocat*	= the girl is calling the sailor.
2.	*agricola*	*patriam*	*amat*	= the farmer loves (his) fatherland.
3.	*fēmina*	*deam*	*laudat*	= the woman praises the goddess.
4.	*nauta*	*aquam*	*nōn amat*	= the sailor does not love water.
5.	*nauta*	*īnsulam*	*habitat*	= the sailor inhabits (lives in) the island.
6.	*puella*	*ancillās*	*vocat*	= the girl is calling the maid-servants.

Exercise 2.12

	S	V	O
1.	<u>Laelia</u>	calls the	<u>girl</u>.
	S	O	
	Laelia	*puellam*	
2.	<u>Sulpicia</u>	does not like	<u>poets</u>.
	S	O	
	Sulpicia	*poētās*	
3.	The <u>girls</u>	watch the	<u>maid-servants</u>.
	S	O	
	puellae	*ancillās*	
4.	<u>Sulpicia</u>	praises	the <u>farmer</u>.
	S	O	
	Sulpicia	*agricolam*	
5.	The <u>sailors</u>	kill	the <u>farmer</u>.
	S	O	
	nautae	*agricolam*	

Exercise 2.13

	S	V	O		S	O	V
1.	The woman	loves	the daughter	=	fēmina	fīliam	amat.
2.	Laelia	loves	the goddess	=	Laelia	deam	amat.
3	The farmer	murders	a maid-servant	=	agricola	ancillam	necat.
4.	Sulpicia	calls	the sailor	=	Sulpicia	nautam	vocat.
5.	The sailor	loves	islands	=	nauta	īnsulās	amat.
6.	The goddess	watches	the girls	=	dea	puellās	spectat.
7.	The poet	does not praise the inhabitants		=	poēta	incolās	nōn laudat.
8.	The girl	calls	the poets	=	puella	poētās	vocat.

Exercise 2.14

	S	O	V			O	S	V
1.	agricolae	īnsulam	habitant.		4.	fīliam	fēmina	spectat.

1. The farmers inhabit (live in) the island.
4. The woman watches the daughter.

	O	S	V			S	O	V
2.	deam	puella	amat.		5.	puellae	rēgīnam	laudant.

2. The girl loves the goddess.
5. The girls praise the queen.

	S	O	V			O	S	V
3.	ancillae	poētam	vocant.		6.	rēgīnam	puellae	laudant.

3. The maid-servants are calling the poet.
6. The girls praise the queen.

Exercise 2.15

	S	V
1.	fēminae	spectant.

1. The women are watching.

	O	V + S
2.	fēminās	spectant.

2. They are watching the women.

3.

O	S	V
nautās	*agricola*	*laudat.*

The farmer praises the sailors.

4.

O	V + S
agricolam	*laudant.*

They praise the farmer.

5.

S	O	V
puellae	*patriam*	*amant.*

The girls love (their) fatherland.

Exercise 2.16

1. Cassia and Sulpicia are singing; a sailor calls Cassia and asks "Cassia, why are you singing?" A farmer calls Sulpicia and asks "Why are you singing, Sulpicia?" Cassia no longer sings. The sailor calls Cassia again; the sailor praises Cassia because she is no longer singing. Sulpicia no longer sings. The farmer calls Sulpicia and the farmer praises the woman because she is no longer singing. A poet enters; the poet calls Sulpicia and Cassia; the poet asks the girl and the woman "Why are you not singing?" Cassia and Sulpicia sing again; the sailor does not praise the girl; the farmer does not praise the woman; the poet, however, praises the girl and the woman.

2.   (a) *cantō; rogō.*
  (b) Vocative.
  (c) *Cassiam.*
  (d) *poētae.*
  (e) It would be *cantās.*

Chapter 3

On names

Most Roman men had three names. The first was the *praenōmen* (fore-name) chosen by their parents. There was only a handful of common *praenōmina*; they all ended in '*–us*'. The boys and men in this course are always referred to by their *praenōmina*.

Next came the *nōmen*, which was the name of the *gēns* or clan to which one belonged; this always ended in '*-ius*'. Then came the *cognōmen* which gave the name of one's family within the clan.

Thus we have *Lūcius Cornēlius Sulla.* Men were generally referred to by their *cognōmen,* e.g. *Sulla* or *Cicerō,* whose name in full was *Mārcus Tullius Cicerō.* The *praenōmina* had recognised abbreviations. We used to have to learn these, copying them from Kennedy's Latin Primer, but for those who have mislaid their copy of this trusty tome, here are the more common ones:

A.	*Aulus*
C.	*Gāius*
Cn.	*Gnaeus*
D.	*Decimus*
L.	*Lūcius*
M.	*Mārcus*
M'	*Mānius*
P.	*Publius*
Q.	*Quīntus*
Ser.	*Servius*
S.	*Sextus*
Sp.	*Spurius*
Tib./Ti.	*Tiberius*
T.	*Titus*

The *cognōmen* often ended in '*a*' as with *Sulla* and *L. Sergius Catilīna* and *Ser. (Servius) Sulpicius Galba.* These *cognōmina* are all 1st declension, masculine. Women were known by the feminine form of their *nōmen*, e.g. *Līvia, Clōdia.*

On quantities

I know it is asking a lot to expect pupils to learn the quantities of words even as they learn the words themselves. But for those who will continue at a later date to study Latin, if they have been taught to take quantities seriously from the start, this will vastly increase their enjoyment of Latin poetry. Again, if they read aloud, as I hope they will do, it is important that they should know the rules of stress in a Latin word, and will stress mightily the penultimate syllable when it is long and the ante-penultimate if there is one, when the penultimate is short, but hardly ever the last syllable (except in a monosyllable!). I thought that setting this out on paper and propounding the two types of long syllables (i.e. long by nature and long by position) would not increase a young pupil's enthusiasm for the subject! But I hope that this can be got across orally. Perhaps a helpful way of doing so would be to chant out frequently and sonorously the following sentences:

> *Lū́cĭus et Tī́tus, púĕrī mágnī, Rōmā́nī érant.*
>
> *Sulpícĭa et Laélĭa, puéllae púlchrae Rōmā́nae érant.*
>
> *égo mágnus et púlcher Británnĭam hábĭtō; Británnus sum;* or
>
> *égo mágna et púlchra Británnĭam hábĭtō; Británna sum.*

One of the hardest things to get across, I find, is the difference between long by nature and long by position. It might be useful if I set out the following: in a word like *portant* both syllables scan long. They are long because the vowel in them is in each case followed by more than one consonant. In other words, they scan long because of the position of the vowels in them. But the vowels themselves are usually *not* long, in which case they should not be pronounced as long.

In *vīdī*, however, both syllables scan long, but this time it is because both 'i's are long by nature. The length of these syllables has nothing whatever to do with the position of the vowels, and the vowels should be pronounced long.

Sometimes a syllable can be longer than ever, the vowel in it both being long by nature and standing before two or more consonants. An example of this is the first syllable of *nūntiō*. This is called a concealed or hidden quantity. In such a case the vowel in the syllable should be pronounced long in accordance with its natural length.

How do we then detect a hidden quantity? A vowel before 'ns' and 'nf' is long, even if the 's' or 'f' are in different words: e.g. *īn scūtō*. The vowel before '-sc' in a verb in '-scō' is regularly long, e.g. *crēscō*. We are told a number of hidden quantities by Cicero and there are other ways of tracking them down given (pp. 65-75) in '*Vōx Latīna*' by Prof. W. Sidney Allen (C.U.P., 2nd ed. 1978), the 'bible' of Latin pronunciation.* A few typical words with unpredictable hidden quantities are *stēlla* (a star), *frūstrā* (in vain) and *ēst* (he or she eats), not to be confused with *est* (he, she or it is).

If a short vowel stands before two consonants, the second of which is 'r' or 'l', the syllable is regulalry regarded as short. E.g. *ímpĕtrō*. But if the vowel is followed by 'rr' or 'll', the syllable is long. E.g. *libéllus*.

Finally, 'h' doesn't count as a consonant, and 'x' is a double consonant. Ah, well; it's all part of the fun.

* N.B. I must admit that I have not followed Allen's exposition on quantities and lengths here (*op. cit.* pp. 89-92). I have shamelessly used the word 'quantity' to mean long or short, and I talk of long and short syllables. I have also preferred elsewhere to stick to the traditional terminology of which Allen disapproves. After all, the whole point of the whole thing is that a **long** syllable, theoretically at least, should take **longer** to pronounce than a **short** one. The terms 'heavy' and 'light' obscure this fundamental issue.

Exercise 3.1

1. *agricolae hastae* (or *hastās*).
2. *agricolārum hasta* (or *hastam*).
3. *agricolārum hastae* (or *hastās*).
4. *Claudiae fīlia* (or *fīliam*).
5. *Claudiae fīliae* (or *fīliās*).
6. *Quīntī fīliī* (or *filiōs*).*

*We apologise for the inadvertent appearance of these 2nd declension nouns at this stage.

Exercise 3.2

1.	*agricolae*	6.	*Sulpiciā*
2.	*ancillārum*	7.	*Laeliam*
3.	*hastae*	8.	*Cassiae*
4.	*īnsulās*	9.	*incolīs*
5.	*fīliae*	10.	*nautīs*

Exercise 3.3

1.	*puellārum*	6.	*Sulpiciae*
2.	*puellae*	7.	*Cassia*
3.	*fēminae*	8.	*Cassiam*
4.	*fēminārum*	9.	*sagittā*
5.	*ō Laelia*	10.	*sagittīs*

Exercise 3.4

1. The women love (their) daughters;
   or, They love the daughters of the woman.
2. The queen calls the maid-servants.
3. The farmers give spears to the sailors.
4. O, farmers, the girl is singing.
5. The poets are telling a story;*
   or, They are telling the story of the poet;
   or, They are telling a story to the poet.
6. They are praising the queen's maid-servants;
   or, The queens are praising the maid-servants.
7. The sailors are carrying spears;
   or, They are carrying the sailor's spears.
8. The farmers' daughters are hurrying.
9. They do not love the fatherland.
10. The sailors inhabit (live in) the island;
    or, They inhabit (live in) the sailor's island.

*With apologies for the inadvertent appearance of *nārrō* (= I tell) and *fābula* (= story). These words are given on page 24 of the pupil's book, but are not in the level 1 syllabus.

Exercise 3.5

1. The farmers and the sailors are fighting; the farmers are fighting with spears and the sailors (are fighting) with arrows. The queen of the island gives money to the farmers and to the sailors; they fight no longer. Sulpicia is a woman; Cassia is a girl. They watch the farmers and the sailors. Soon Sulpicia and Cassia fight. They fight for a long time and at last Sulpicia cries out (lit. shouts) "Where is the money? The queen gives money to the farmers and to the sailors. She is queen of women and girls also. However, the queen does not give money to a woman and a girl." "O queen," cries (lit. shouts) Cassia, "you do not love women and girls! We, therefore, do not love the queen!"

2. (a) *rēgīna (Sulpicia, fēmina, Cassia, puella, pecūnia)*
   (b) *agricolae (nautae)*
   (c) *pecūniam (rēgīnam)*
   (d) *agricolās (nautās, fēminās, puellās)*

(e) *īnsulae*

(f) *fēminārum (puellārum)*

(g) *fēminae (puellae)*

(h) *agricolīs (nautīs)*

(i) *hastīs (sagittīs)*

(j) *rēgīna* (in line 9); elsewhere *rēgīna* is nom. sing.

Exercise 3.6

1. maid-servant
2. *–ae*
3. f.
4. *fīlia*
5. *–ae*
6. *īnsula*
7. f.
8. *–ae*
9. m.
10. inhabitant

Exercise 3.7

1. *amīcī*
2. *equīs*
3. *cibō*
4. *ō Mārce*
5. *ō servī*
6. *ventum*
7. *mūrī*
8. *mūrōrum*
9. *equō*
10. *servōrum*

Exercise 3.8

1. *Mārcus servum spectat.*
2. *amīcus cibum parat.*
3. *ancilla dominum laudat.*
4. *Mārcus ancillam amat.*
5. *servus mūrum aedificat.*
6. *Aule, quis equōs spectat?*
7. *servī hīc sunt.*
8. *servī hīc sunt.*
9. *ubi est Quīntī equus?*
10. *Aule, cūr nōn labōrās?*

Exercise 3.9

Hercules (Heracles in Greek) was the great hero of the ancient world. He was the son of Jupiter by a human mother Alcmena. He himself was human, but was endowed with superhuman strength. He performed many heroic tasks, ridding the world of cruel monsters. His most famous exploits were the Twelve Labours imposed on him by King Eurystheus. He was pretty short-tempered and according to one story, is supposed to have killed Linus, his music-teacher, with a blow from a cithara for having rebuked him too sharply. Dare we tell our pupils this story?

1.   (a) We are told that he is a Thracian and that he is a master of mares.
   (b) Diomedes gave boys, girls, women and men, who were his guests, as food to his mares.
   (c) He called the inhabitants.
   (d) He did not praise Diomedes and he did not like him.
   (e) He was carrying out one of his labours (see title of piece).
   (f) He killed him first (in the kinder version!).
   (g) They got their master, Diomedes, to eat.

2. Diomedes is Thracian; he is a master of mares. Diomedes gives food to his mares; the mares gobble up boys, girls, women and men, who are (their) master's guests. A man enters Thrace. He is a Greek. He calls the inhabitants and asks "Why do the master's mares gobble up the guests? I do not praise the master; I do not like the master of the mares. The inhabitants ask "Who are you?" "I am Hercules," he shouts, "and I am labouring here. Where is Diomedes?" "Diomedes is here," cry (lit. shout) the inhabitants. Soon Hercules kills the master and gives the master to the mares. Thus the mares gobble up their master and thus Hercules tames (lit. overcomes) both master and mares.

3. (a) gen. pl.
   (b) dat. pl.
   (c) *rogō* = I ask or ask for
   (d) nom. pl
   (e) (i)   *cibum, Thrāciam, dominum* (any two of these)
       (ii) *puerōs, puellās, fēminās, virōs, incolās, convīvās, equās* (any two of these)

Exercise 3.10

1. *liber, librī,* m. = book

	Singular	**Plural**
Nominative	*liber*	*librī*
Vocative	*liber*	*librī*
Accusative	*librum*	*librōs*
Genitive	*librī*	*librōrum*
Dative	*librō*	*librīs*
Ablative	*librō*	*librīs*

2. *ager, agrī,* m. = field

	Singular	**Plural**
Nominative	*ager*	*agrī*
Vocative	*ager*	*agrī*
Accusative	*agrum*	*agrōs*
Genitive	*agrī*	*agrōrum*
Dative	*agrō*	*agrīs*
Ablative	*agrō*	*agrīs*

Exercise 3.11

1. The boys are building walls.
2. The farmers and the sailors are shouting.
3. Marcus, where is the teacher's friend?
4. The women are preparing food for the boys.
5. The maid-servants do not like winds.
6. The teachers' horses are hurrying.
7. The poet is giving a book to Cassia.
8. The masters are killing the slaves with spears;
   or, They are killing the master's slaves with spears.
9. The farmers love the horse;
   or, They love the farmer's horse.
10. Farmers, where are Cassia and Laelia?

Exercise 3.12

1. *Aulus puerō aquam dat.*
2. *puer et puella labōrant.*
3. *servī mūrum aedificant.*
4. *poētae deam amant.*
5. *Cassia et Sulpicia magistrō cantant.*
6. *magistrī servī cibum equīs dant.*
7. *dominōrum servī nōn labōrant, sed clāmant.*
8. *puellae Aulī equōs amant.*
9. *Quīnte, ubi sunt servī?*
10. *nōn festīnant: ambulant.*

Exercise 3.13

1. *puerī et puellae hastās ancillīs dant.*
2. *puellae et equī nautīs cantant.*
3. *ubi sunt ventī et patriae?*
4. *agricolae ambulant et labōrant.*
5. *nautae labōrant et ambulant.*
6. *agricolae et nautae nōn ambulant, sed labōrant.*
7. *nautae et agricolae nōn labōrant, sed ambulant.*
8. *domine, poētae amīcī incolās librīs necant.*
9. *incolae hīc sunt.*
10. *nōn sunt.*

Exercise 3.14

1. labour
2. library
3. patriotic
4. nautical
5. dominate
6. agriculture
7. equestrian
8. puerile
9. amicable
10. vocative

Exercise 3.15

1. Poets love the gods.
2. O Marcus, where are the farmer's horses?
3. The goddesses are giving water to the inhabitants.
4. The maid-servants of the goddesses are girls.
5. O (my) son, the food is here; or there is food here.

Chapter 4

On ā/ab = by

This meaning of *'ā' (ab)* is given in vocabularies; but it only means 'by' when followed by a living agent; e.g. *ab amīcō* = 'by a friend'. However, we have not for the moment held it necessary to go into this. We shall say more about it when we come to the Passive Voice.

On the imperfect and past tenses

The version 'I was singing' for *cantābam* is only really appropriate if it is followed by, say, 'when he entered'. The 'used to sing' version would generally over-accentuate the idea of frequency. Whereas Latin uses the imperfect to recount events which took place over a lengthy period or which constituted a state or condition rather than an act, we in English use a simple past tense in such cases. I had a 'profound theory' about this English use of the past tense to translate these Latin imperfects but, alas, the more I thought about it the less true it seemed. For the moment, suffice it to say that although 'I was doing' or 'I used to do' are not always the best ways to translate a Latin imperfect, these translations have the merit of driving home the fact that the imperfect is not the same as the past. To teach the tense as meaning 'I did' (e.g. I sang) would be most unhelpful. At a later date we may gradually tell the truth which, at this early stage, as so often, would be far too muddling.

Exercise 4.1

1. *verbum, -ī*, n. = word

	Singular	Plural
Nominative	verb**um**	verb**a**
Vocative	verbum	verba
Accusative	verb**um**	verba
Genitive	verbī	verbōrum
Dative	verbō	verbīs
Ablative	verbō	verbīs

2. *templum, -ī*, n. = temple

	Singular	Plural
Nominative	templ**um**	templ**a**
Vocative	templum	templa
Accusative	templ**um**	templa
Genitive	templī	templōrum
Dative	templō	templīs
Ablative	templō	templīs

3. *oppidum, -ī*, n. = town

	Singular	**Plural**
Nominative	*oppid**um***	*oppid**a***
Vocative	*oppidum*	*oppida*
Accusative	*oppid**um***	*oppid**a***
Genitive	*oppidī*	*oppidōrum*
Dative	*oppidō*	*oppidīs*
Ablative	*oppidō*	*oppidīs*

Exercise 4.2

1. The boys are entering the temple.
2. The sailors are watching the towns.
3. The temple of the goddess is here.
4. The inhabitant is watching towns and temples.
5. Farmers do not love words;
    or, They do not love the farmer's words.

Exercise 4.3

1. *Quīntus verba agricolārum laudat.*
2. *Mārcus et agricolae templum aedificant.*
3. *templum hīc est.*
4. *Aulus et Laelia templum intrant.*
5. *cūr bellum est?*

Exercise 4.4

1. Gnaeus and Sextus are in the island.
2. Cassia sings with her (boy-)friend.
3. The boys are walking from the fields.
4. Laelia is hurrying from the goddess' temple.
5. The poet is singing about girls.
6. Sulpicia is giving food down from the wall to the sailors.
7. Aulus works in the field.
8. The sailor's sons are walking out of the water.
9. The girls are hurrying from the waves.
10. The boys are not walking with the maid-servants.

Exercise 4.5

1. *cum amīcō ambulō.*
2. *nautae dē templō festīnant.*
3. *cum agricolā labōrō.*
4. *ō Mārce, quis in aquā ambulat?*
5. *fēminae ex īnsulā festīnant.*
6. *agricolae in agrīs nōn labōrant.*
7. *puerī de puellīs cantant.*
8. *ancillae ab agrō ambulant.*

Exercise 4.6

1. (a) It is being attacked by sailors.
   (b) They do not like its dangers.
   (c) They carry shields.
   (d) Quintus and Lucius hurry out from the temple with their friends.
   (e) They are not at all effective as defenders of the town.
   (f) The gods.
   (g) They free horses from (their) stables; and the horses rush (lit. hurry) out of the town and overcome the sailors.
   (h) Not at all.
   (i) That they fought with words rather than (lit. not) with deeds.

2. There is a war, and sailors are attacking the town; Marcus and Sextus are in the town; they do not like the dangers of war. They carry shields and watch the sailors down from the wall. Soon Quintus and Lucius, poets, hurry out of the temple with their friends; the poets do not fight with the sailors; there is no (lit. not a) battle. Marcus and Sextus ask for help from the gods and free horses from (their) stables; the horses rush (lit. hurry) out of the town and overcome the sailors. Quintus sings about the war: "We poets overcome the sailors." The poets fight with words, not with deeds.

3. (a) It is in the accusative. It is the object of *oppugnant.*
   (b) It is in the accusative. It is the object of *amant.*
   (c) Genitive = of war.
   (d) *scūtum.*
   (e) It would become *mūrīs.*
   (f) It is in the nominative.
   (g) The sailors. Nautical means connected with sailors.
   (h) It would become *festīnat.*
   (i) *in oppidō* = in the town.
      dē mūrō = down from the wall.
      cum amīcīs = with (their) friends.
      ex templō = out of the temple.
      cum nautīs = with the sailors.
      ā dīs = from the gods.
      ex stabulīs = out of (their) stables.
      ex oppidō = out of the town.
      dē bellō = about the war.

Exercise 4.7

1. *altum*
2. *fessīs*
3. *magnō*
4. *laetōs*
5. *novae*
6. *parvīs*
7. *saeve*
8. *tūtās*
9. *multa*
10. *malīs*

Exercise 4.8

1. *in magnō perīculō*
2. *malī servī*
3. *ō bonī nautae*
4. *ex magnā īnsulā*
5. *fessō agricolae*
6. *in proeliō magnō*
7. *cum incolīs bonīs*
8. *ex altā aquā*
9. *īrātī dominī*
10. *laetōs dominōs*

Exercise 4.9

1. In war-time (lit. wars) boys are not safe.
2. We are happy; the new teacher is not savage.
3. Good masters do not like bad slaves;
   or, They do not like the bad slaves of the good master.
4. O good friend, we are in great danger.
5. The little girls are tired.
6. Happy women like good words;
   or, They like the good words of the happy woman.
7. The new temple is big.
8. The sailors are tired; they are sailing in deep waves.

Exercise 4.10

1. *servus malus est.*
2. *nauta īrātus est.*
3. *agricolae fessī sunt.*
4. *saevī nautae puerōs sagittīs superant.*
5. *fēminae laetae bonās ancillās amant.*
6. *magistrī de altō templō ambulant.*
7. *ō parve puer, ubi sunt parvae puellae?*
8. *agricolae et nautae sociī in magnā īnsulā sunt.*
9. *dominī multum aurum bonīs poētīs dant.*
10. *Lūcius bonī magistrī fīlius est.*

Exercise 4.11

1. Novelty
2. Magnitude
3. Society
4. Dominate
5. Multiply

Exercise 4.12

1. *intrābam*
2. *laudābās*
3. *Sextus nāvigābat*
4. *cantābāmus*
5. *portābātis*
6. *dabant*

Exercise 4.13

1. Great men used to kill savage inhabitants.
2. The good teacher used to praise good poets.
3. Happy farmers were standing in the high fields.
4. Weary women were hurrying from the big wall.
5. Because they were wicked, Sextus and Gnaeus used to fight with girls.
6. Because the farmers were tired, they were not working in the fields.
7. The savage sailors were attacking a small island.
8. The boys were carrying the food (together) with good girls.

Exercise 4.14

1. *nautae in altīs undīs nāvigābant.*
2. *agricolae dē magnīs agrīs festīnābant.*
3. *puerī parvī in templō cantābant.*
4. *laetae fēminae bonās puellās laudābant.*
5. *incolae cibum bonīs nūntiīs dabant.*
6. *dea magna in īnsulā habitābat.*
7. *malī virī nautās gladiīs superābant.*
8. *servus saevus pecūniam amat.*

Exercise 4.15

1. The farmers do not love the horses;
   or, They do not love the farmer's horses.
2. The sailors were entering the islands.
3. The girls were tired.
4. The farmer's son was small.
5. The crowd was savage.
6. The bad boys were in the street;
   or, There were bad boys in the street.
7. The queen was praising the girls.
8. The good teacher is praising the boys.
9. The savage sailors were entering the field;
   or, They were entering the savage sailor's field.
10. A good master loves (his) slaves.

Exercise 4.16

1. *fēmina in viā stat.*
2. *rēgīnam magnam amāmus.*
3. *agricolae in agrīs labōrant.*
4. *puellae fessīs equīs cibum dabant.*
5. *puerī aquās spectābant.*
6. *malī virī incolās necābant.*
7. *nautae gladiōs nōn portābant.*
8. *sociōs laudābāmus.*
9. *parvae puellae fessae erant.*
10. *novus liber magnus est.*

Exercise 4.17

I must admit that my synopsis of Homer's *Odyssey* scarcely does the epic full justice. Perhaps, however there is just a chance that it may move someone to get hold of a good translation. I remember how much I loved stories from Homer, when I was a boy.

Our artist has been incredibly kind to Penelope after all those long years! I've always thought of her as something of a blue-stocking, who took ages to accept that Odysseus really was Odysseus. Compare his old dog Argos and his nurse Eurycleia who knew the truth immediately for all his disguise!

Unfortunately I could not bring them in, as *canis* is 3rd declension and so is *nūtrīx*.

1.   (a) Ulysses was attacking Troy.
       (b) No, because he was in great danger.
       (c) We learn that Ulysses was not the sort of person to be overcome by many dangers.
       (d) No, we are told in line 3 that he sailed in savage and deep waves.
       (e) The ghosts of dead men and of dead women.
       (f) The goddess Minerva.
       (g) As tired, but happy.
       (h) That she was happy and that Ulysses lived with her for a long time.

2.   Ulysses was Greek; he attacked Troy for a long time; then he wandered for a long time and was in great danger; however the many dangers did not overcome the man. He sailed in savage and deep waves; he also looked upon (lit. watched) the ghosts of dead men and of dead women. The goddess Minerva loved the man. At last, therefore, tired but happy he entered his own island, Ithaca; he lived for a long time in the island with his happy wife.

N.B. We have translated the imperfects in the above passage by the English past (see page 18). In line 7 the past tense *intrāvit* decribes a quickly completed act.

3.   (a) imperfect; *oppugnābant*
       (b) *magnum perīculum*
       (c) *multa:* nominative plural
       (d) *undīs*
       (e) *spectat*
       (f) nominative
       (g) *intrābat*
       (h) *marītā*

On Graecus = "a Greek man"

This might be a good point to tell our pupils the effect of using an adjective on its own, without a noun: *Graecus*, used alone, in the masculine, means "a Greek man'. *Graeca*, used on its own, in the feminine, means a Greek woman. Similarly *bonī* = good men, *pulchrae* = beautiful women, *multī* = many people, etc.

Chapter 5

On the perfect tense

This tense I find the most worrying of all. I don't really like calling it the perfect tense, because at least half the time it isn't perfect at all. But the tradition of giving it this name is so strong that I have succumbed to it. I find it utterly baffling that the Romans, who had such a formidable array of tenses and who took sequence of tenses so seriously, should have produced this two-headed monster, which could be either primary (perfect) or historic (past). Even the Greeks who were far more easy-going with tenses and sequences had a perfectly (sorry!) good perfect and a totally distinct aorist (or past) tense. Still we must grin and bear it and do our best to cope. But I do draw the line at the name 'perfect without 'have''. One might just as well talk about showers without water or violins without strings. We must do our best from the general context to decide whether we are dealing with a perfect or a past, and generally, but by no means always, this is not too terrible. Still, in my translations I have tried to remind pupils over and over again, of the ambiguity of this form, so that awareness of this should become second nature to them.

On the imperfect and past tenses (again)

My research into the difference between the past tense and the imperfect has almost turned me into a battered wreck, all the more so because I thought that I had some illuminating views on this subject; my general idea was based on the fact that the English past tense should frequently be translated by the imperfect in Latin, and *vice versa*. In fact, this does follow logically from my piece on page 18 on the imperfect and past tenses; in other words, if the English past tense is actually referring to a state or condition, the translation should be into the imperfect. For example in translating 'you who all felt the same' into Latin, we should happily say *'vōs, quī omnēs idem sentiēbātis'*, following in Cicero's footsteps (*post reditum in senatu* xi, 29). All my faith in this was destroyed by a line in Ovid *'dōnec erās simplex, animum cum corpore amāvī'* (*Amores*, 1, x, 13). The whole thing seems to cry aloud for *'amābam'*; the verb is describing a continuous state of mind. This form *amāvī* occurs elsewhere in Ovid and Cicero where it is really hard to explain. The only thing I can say about this is that where the imperfect is used, it focuses on the state or condition involved, but where the past is used, it focuses on the fact that such and such occurred.

At least the past tense in English can *very often* be translated into the Latin imperfect correctly, and so can the Latin imperfect be translated into the English past. (I have done this once or twice – see Exercise 8.2 no. 8.).

On in + accusative

This may be the time to tell our pupils that if you are going, say, to a place, intending to enter it, then the English 'to' should be translated by *'in'* with the accusative, whereas *ad* + accusative would mean 'to the neighbourhood of', or just 'towards'. But if you are going to a town or small island, mentioned by name, you use the accusative alone, without a preposition.

> E.g.   *Rōmam festīnō* = I am hurrying to Rome.
> *Monam nāvigō* = I am sailing to the Isle of Man.

Exercise 5.1

1. Three women are standing on the wall.
2. Four boys were shouting.
3. One farmer was watching the horses.
4. Ten girls live in the island.
5. Seven sailors were sailing.
6. Two maid-servants are singing about the goddess.
7. Five books are in the temple;
   or, There are five books in the temple.
8. Nine horses are walking out of the waves.
9. Six men were praising the poet.
10. Eight good slaves are working.

Exercise 5.2

1. *quattuor et quīnque novem sunt.*
2. *quīnque et trēs octō sunt.*
3. *duo et quattuor sex sunt.*
4. *quīnque et quīnque decem sunt.*
5. *quattuor et trēs septem sunt.*

Exercise 5.3

1. *novem servī labōrābant.*
2. *decem incolae in īnsulā habitābant.*
3. *ūna puella in agrō stat.*
4. *septem puerī cantābant.*
5. *duo virī poētam laudant.*
6. *sex fēminae in templō erant.*
7. *trēs equī ex undīs festīnābant.*
8. *octō equī in agrō stant.*

Exercise 5.4

1. (a) Fourteen.
   (b) Two.
   (c) Because Latona's children were a god and a goddess.
   (d) She was carried by winds to (Mount) Sipylus.
   (e) A rock.

2. Niobe had seven sons and seven daughters; once upon a time, Niobe boasted thus "Latona has one son and one daughter; Niobe has seven daughters (together) with seven sons". Latona was very (lit. greatly) angry. The son of Latona was Phoebus Apollo and the daughter (was) Diana. Phoebus Apollo slew Niobe's seven sons with arrows and similarly (lit. thus) Diana slew (her) daughters. Finally (lit. at last) winds carried Niobe through the sky to (Mount) Sipylus. There Niobe has become (lit. is) a rock, and there is always water in the eyes of the rock. Niobe is always weeping.

3. (a) Because its subject *(fīliae)* is plural.
   (b) Ablative; with arrows.
   (c) Accusative; daughters (as objects of the verb).
   (d) It would be *portat.*
   (e) It would be *lacrimābat.*

Exercise 5.5

1. Aulus has walked from the temple;
   or, Aulus walked from the temple.
2. Gnaeus and Sextus hurried into the waves;
   or, Gnaeus and Sextus have hurried into the waves.
3. Where are the boys? They have entered the temple.
4. The farmers worked in the fields;
   or, The farmers have worked in the fields.
5. Where are the sailors? They have sailed to the island.
6. Sulpicia and Cassia sang;
   or, Sulpicia and Cassia have sung

Exercise 5.6

1. *ubi sunt nautae? trāns undās nāvigāvērunt.*
2. *per magnum agrum festīnāvimus.*
3. *poētās laudāvistis.*
4. *in templum multōs librōs portāvērunt.*
5. *cantāvistī.*
6. *cantāvistī.*

Exercise 5.7

Here I think I should have added the sequel to the story given. Proserpina's mother Ceres sought everywhere for her daughter unsuccessfully. But in the end, an agreement was reached whereby Proserpina spent part of the year on Earth and part in the Underworld.

I have marked the *'o'* of *Prōserpina* long, having found it so in Virgil and in Ovid. Really it should be *'ō' or 'ŏ'*, but I have been trying to go easy, for the time being, on ambiguous quantities.

In line 4 of my story, *'amāvit'* brings out the fact of Pluto's loving Proserpina, whereas in line 8 *amābat* concentrates on Proserpina's state of mind or feelings.

1. (a) Proserpina is the daughter of the goddess, Cerēs. She was a good, (lit. and) beautiful and happy girl.
   (b) A god, master of the Underworld.
   (c) He was watching the girls.
   (d) He loved Proserpina. He carried (off) the girl into the Underworld.
   (e) Because the Underworld was not a good place, but (was) bad and savage.

2. Ceres is a goddess. Proserpina is the goddess' daughter. Proserpina was a good (lit. and) beautiful and happy girl. Once upon a time she was walking in the fields with (her) friends. Pluto, a god, master of the Underworld, watched the girls and loved Proserpina. The god carried the girl into the Underworld; there Proserpina became (lit. was) the queen. However the Underworld was not a good place but (was) bad and savage. Therefore because Proserpina loved beautiful fields and happy earth and fair (lit. good) winds, she was miserable there.

N.B. Whereas we say 'good, beautiful and happy', in Latin one says either 'good and beautiful and happy' or 'good, beautiful, happy'.

3. (a) genitive
    (b) perfect
    (c) accusative
    (d) nominative
    (e) *in agrīs* = in the fields
        cum amīcīs = with (her) friends
        in Tartarum = into the Underworld
    (f) *erat* = was (four times)
        ambulābat = was walking
        spectābat = was watching
        amābat = loved
    (g) *pulcher ager*
    (h) *miserae*

Exercise 5.8

1.	puerile	4.	miserable
2.	master	5.	ventilate
3.	local	6.	contrary

Exercise 5.9

1. When Aulus and (his) friends are working, they often sing.
2. When Claudia and Cassia worked, they were happy.
3. Even farmers used to sing.
4. Soon the inhabitants gave much gold to the poets.
5. Therefore the poets were glad.
6. Therefore the poets were glad.
7. The weary maid-servants were walking for a long time.
8. The savage sailors immediately fought with the inhabitants.
9. Then the queen was praising the women again.
10. There the good master was giving good food to (his) slaves.

Exercise 5.10

1. *puella equum amat.*
2. *nauta fēminam vocāvit.*
3. *agricola agrum spectāvit.*
4. *servus magnum mūrum aedificat.*
5. *dea virum amat.*
6. *dominus aurum in templum portābat.*
7. *in agrīs labōrābās.*
8. *oppidum oppugnābāmus.*
9. *magister puerum laudāvit.*
10. *dea caelum habitat.*

Exercise 5.11

1.   (a) With spears.
     (b) They hurried into the temple.
     (c) Because they loved the horse. (They asked the god for help (lit. asked for help from the god).)
     (d) As good and strong.
     (e) With the wine which they gave them.
     (f) By making them drunk.
     (g) Safe.

2.   Once upon a time on the island (some) savage inhabitants tried to kill a horse with spears. Because they loved the horse, Marcus and Sextus hurried into the temple, and when they were in the temple, they asked the god for help (lit. asked for help from the god). "O god," they cried (lit. shouted) "we ask for help against the wicked inhabitants." The god was good and strong, and he gave the boys wine; the boys gave the wine to the inhabitants and thus they overcame the inhabitants. And when the boys overcame the inhabitants with wine, the horse was safe.

3.   (a) Into the temple.
     (b) In the temple.
     (c) Perfect.
     (d) Vocative
     (e) Accusative. It agrees with *incolās* which is governed by *contrā*.
     (f) Nominative.
     (g) Dative.
     (h) Perfect.

N.B. If a noun consists of males and females, as for example *saevī incolae* in line 1 of our passage, the adjective agreeing with it should be masculine – an example, I'm afraid, of Roman political incorrectness.

Exercise 5.12

1.   *vocō, vocāre, vocāvī, vocātum* = I call
2.   *clāmō, clāmāre, clāmāvī, clāmātum* = I shout
3.   *aedificō, aedificāre, aedificāvī, aedificātum* = I build
4.   *ambulō, ambulāre, ambulāvī, ambulātum* = I walk
5.   *pugnō, pugnāre, pugnāvī, pugnātum* = I fight

Exercise 5.13

1.   *aedificō, aedificāre, aedificāvī, aedificātum* = I build
2.   *labōrō, labōrāre, labōrāvī, labōrātum* = I work
3.   *vocō, vocāre, vocāvī, vocātum* = I call
4.   *cantō, cantāre, cantāvī, cantātum* = I sing
5.   *necō, necāre, necāvī, necātum* = I kill, murder

Chapter 6

On respondeō

I have generally translated *respondeō* as 'I reply' rather than 'I answer', because it is followed by the dative of the questioner and not by the accusative.

On questions

Very often a particular stress can be put on the first word in the question, especially if it is unexpected.

For example: *puellane agricolam superāvit?*
                 Was it really a girl who overcame the farmer?

or   *malīne puerī in templō cantābant?*
                 Was it really the bad boys who were singing in the temple?

On easier English into Latin sentences

In Chapters 6-8 there will be sentences that conform rigidly to the Level 1 syllabus requirement for English into Latin (see page 1). We are committed to encouraging pupils to translate into Latin throughout the course, even where it involves working beyond the confines of the syllabus, as it is such a valuable teaching tool for the Latin – English work.

Exercise 6.1

1.   *dēleō, dēlēs, dēlet, dēlēmus, dēlētis, dēlent*
2.   *timēbam, timēbās, timēbat, timēbāmus, timēbātis, timēbant*
3.   *tenuī, tenuistī, tenuit, tenuimus, tenuistis, tenuērunt*
4.   *videō, vidēs, videt, vidēmus, vidētis, vident*
5.   *respondēbam, respondēbās, respondēbat, respondēbāmus, respondēbātis, respondēbant*
6.   *mōvī, mōvistī, mōvit, mōvimus, mōvistis, mōvērunt*

Exercise 6.2

1.   deletion = erasure from sense of destruction (*dēleō* = I destroy)
2.   mansion = large house, from idea of somewhere to stay (*maneō* = I remain, stay)
3.   vision = sight (*videō* = I see)
4.   motion = movement (*moveō* = I move (transitive))
5.   station = somewhere where something stops or comes to a stand, i.e. halts (*stō* = I stand)

These English words come from the supines of the Latin words mentioned.

Exercise 6.3

1. The masters warn the inhabitants of (lit. about) war.
2. The teacher orders the boy to reply.
3. The slaves are moving the shields into the fields.
4. Cassia is afraid of (lit. fears) the poet.
5. Aulus, a strong man, does not fear boys.
6. The teacher's daughters, Sulpicia and Laelia, were terrified.
7. The little girls have beautiful books.
8. They gave (or have given) food to Lucius, a good boy.

Exercise 6.4

1. (a) A savage one.
   (b) To move a beautiful, large and tall statue from the town into the temple.
   (c) Their master's anger.
   (d) It frightened them.
   (e) He saw them and shouted "Why have you not lifted the statue?"
   (f) Not at all.
   (g) It flew to the ground and was destroyed.

2. Laurel and Hardy, (who were) friends, had a brutal (lit. savage) master. (This) master ordered the friends to move a beautiful, large and tall statue from the town into the temple; the friends often tried to lift the statue, but (they did so) in vain. Two girls, Sulpicia and Laelia, warned the friends about (their) master's anger and frightened the friends because they greatly feared (their) master. The angry master sees the friends and shouts "Why have you not lifted the statue?" They do not answer. Again and again they try to lift the statue, but the statue always remains in its (own) place. Suddenly they do lift the statue, and immediately they (can) no longer hold (it); the statue flies to the ground. Alas! the friends have destroyed the statue. The master shouts; Sulpicia and Laelia laugh.

3. (a) To dominate is to behave towards someone as a master (*dominus* = master).
   (b) *saevum* agrees with *dominum;*
       pulchram agrees with *statuam;*
       magnam agrees with *statuam;*
       altam agrees with *statuam;*
       īrātus agrees with *dominus;*
       suō agrees with *locō.*
   (c) *movēre* = to move (tr.) or *sublevāre* = to lift.
   (d) It would be *vīdit.*
   (e) *respondērunt.*
   (f) It would be *manēbat.*
   (g) *rīsērunt.*

Exercise 6.5

1. *agricolae scūta dēlēvērunt.*
2. *Claudia, dominī fīlia, in oppidō manet.*
3. *nōs, poētae fīliī, rīdēmus.*
4. *vōs, nautae, saevās undās timētis.*
5. *equī bonī parvās puellās nōn terrent.*
6. *quod bonōs librōs habēmus, laetī sumus.*

7. *librum Aulō, Quīntī fīliō, dedī.*
8. *servōs festīnāre iubent.*

Exercise 6.6

1. The girl frightened (or has frightened) me.
2. The farmer warned (or has warned) you.
3. The sailors ordered (or have ordered) me to hurry.
4. I love you.
5. You do not love me.

Exercise 6.7

1. Boys love (their) fatherland.
2. The farmer gave (or has given) money to his (lit. his own) slaves because they worked (or have worked) in the field.
3. The farmer feared (or has feared) us.
4. He/she/it frightened (or has frightened) the master's good slaves.
5. There was much gold in the goddess' temple.
6. The boys laughed when they hurried down from the wall.
7. We work and watch you.
8. The girls saw (or have seen) the horses;
    or, They saw (or have seen) the girl's horses.

Exercise 6.8

1. *mūrum dēlent.*
2. *agricola agrum videt.*
3. *puer librum tenet.*
4. *dominus multōs amīcōs habet.*
5. *perīculum equum terrēbat.*
6. *Sulpicia et Cassia bellum timent.*
7. *nauta rīdēbat.*
8. *mē monētis.*

Exercise 6.9

1. delete
2. respond
3. terrify
4. timid
5. monitor

Exercise 6.10

1. The boys are not here, but there.
2. The farmers never used to fight with the sailors in the temple.
3. The girls were hurrying to the temple at last.
4. The boys, however, are not hurrying. Where are they?
5. The farmer moved (or has moved) five horses into the fields.
6. The boys were not replying to the teacher because they were afraid.
7. You are working and watching us.
8. You (s.) order the inhabitants to remain in the town.

Exercise 6.11

1. *puer librum movet.*
2. *fēmina puellam monet.*
3. *ancilla pulchram rēgīnam spectābat.*
4. *magister poētam laudat.*
5. *vir īrātus gladium tenet.*
6. *agricolae in agrīs manēbant.*
7. *ex undīs festīnāmus.*
8. *malī virī incolās terruērunt.*

Exercise 6.12

1. Are the boys walking in the street?
2. Are the women carrying the water?
3. Are the maid-servants preparing food?
4. Are sailors afraid of horses?
5. Where are Marcus and Quintus?
6. Who has seen the teachers?
7. What were the men watching?
8. Why are you (pl.) afraid?
9. Were the girls laughing in the fields?
10. Are the boys shouting in the fields?

Exercise 6.13

1.   (a) They are sailing to an island.
     (b) They are working in the fields.
     (c) Where the inhabitants' gold is.
     (d) *iterum.*
     (e) They terrify the inhabitants with swords and spears.
     (f) Because of the inhabitants' words.

2.   Many sailors sail to an island, when the inhabitants are working in the fields. "Where is your gold?" they shout, and when the inhabitants do not reply, they shout again "Where is your gold?" And they terrify the inhabitants with swords and spears. At last the terrified inhabitants reply "It is in our town." Therefore the sailors, happy (now) thanks to (lit. because of) the inhabitants' words, hurry into the town.

It is quite acceptable to treat all these present tenses as historic presents and to translate them with past tenses in English. See the pupil's book, page 32 ("Feeling scholarly?").

3.   (a) Accusative: governed by *ad.*
     (b) *nāvigābant.*
     (c) *respondērunt.*
     (d) *terrēbant.*
     (e) Ablative: in the town.
     (f) Accusative: into the town.

Exercise 6.14

1. (a) *dīcō, dīcis, dīcit, dīcimus, dīcitis, dīcunt* = I say.
    (b) *legēbam, legēbās, legēbat, legēbāmus, legēbātis, legēbant* = I was reading, choosing.
    (c) *scrīpsī, scrīpsistī, scrīpsit, scrīpsimus, scrīpsistis, scrīpsērunt* = I wrote, have written.

2. *dūxī, dūxistī, dūxit, dūximus, dūxistis, dūxērunt*
    lūsī, lūsistī, lūsit, lūsimus, lūsistis, lūsērunt
    discessī, discessistī, discessit, discessimus, discessistis, discessērunt
    ostendī, ostendistī, ostendit, ostendimus, ostendistis, ostendērunt

    (Any three of the above)

Exercise 6.15

1. We are showing (or showed or have shown) the island to the sailor.
2. The boys and girls were reading books.
3. They are playing in the field.
4. Who is leading the women into the temple?
5. Many men are departing out of the town.
6. Quintus, a poet, has written books.
7. The queen of the island ruled the inhabitants;
    or, The queen ruled the inhabitants of the island.
8. Are the women beautiful?
9. Are the masters laughing?
10. Are the masters praising the boys?;
    or, Are they praising the boys of the master?

Exercise 6.16

1. *vir mūrum aedificat.*
2. *puella magistrum laudat.*
3. *poēta gladium timet.*
4. *agricola equum videt.*
5. *servus dominum timet.*
6. *cūr in īnsulā mānsērunt parvī puerī?*
7. *librōsne incolae in oppidō legunt?*
8. *agricolae ab agrīs discēdēbant.*

Exercise 6.17

1. *cūr clāmābās?* (or *clāmābātis?*)
2. *quis cantat?*
3. *parābantne vīnum?*
4. *quis cibum parāvit?*
5. *ubi est vīnum?*
6. *mēne vocāvistī, domine?*
7. *quid puellam terruit?*
8. *quis puerum nōn vīdit?*

Exercise 6.18

1. (a) In Italy.
    (b) King of Alba Longa.
    (c) He overcame him.
    (d) Daughter of Numitor.
    (e) The god of war.

2. Alba Longa is in Italy; it is a town. Proca was king of (lit. ruled) Alba Longa. Numitor and Amulius were sons of Proca. After Proca Numitor was king of Alba Longa. Amulius was wicked. He overcame Numitor and became king of Alba Longa (lit. ruled Alba Longa) himself. Numitor had a daughter, Rhea Silvia. Mars, the god of war, loved Rhea Silvia. Mars and Rhea Silvia had twin sons, Romulus and Remus.

3. (a) It is ablative; it ends in a long *ā* and is governed by *'in'*.
    (b) Perfect.
    (c) *superābat.*.
    (d) Genitive.
    (e) Accusative; they are in apposition to *fīliōs gemellōs,* the objects of *habuērunt.*

N.B. *gemellus* is both an adjective and a noun.

Chapter 7

On the 4th conjugation

In giving only three 4th conjugation verbs, one of which is irregular, I have been faithfully adhering to the syllabus.

Exercise 7.1

1. The teacher is reading the fifth book.
2. Three women were hurrying into the fourth field.
3. The teacher was reading the second book.
4. Who is the tenth son?
5. Are you the ninth son?
6. The master gave (has given) money to the seventh slave.
7. I lived in the eighth street.
8. Where is the sixth shield?
9. The first boy and the third girl were in the temple.
10. Who has read the good poet's book?

Exercise 7.2

1. *veniō, venīs, venit, venīmus, venītis, veniunt*
2. *dormiēbam, dormiēbās, dormiēbat, dormiēbāmus, dormiēbātis, dormiēbant*
3. *vēnī, vēnistī, vēnit, vēnimus, vēnistis, vēnērunt*

Exercise 7.3

1. Quintus' son was watching the sky.
2. Did the girls fear dangers?
3. What did the first boy say? or, What has the first boy said?
4. Why did the masters lead (or, Why have the masters led) the maid-servants out of the temple? or, Why did they lead (or have they led) the master's maid-servants out of the temple?
5. The farmer came into the field, when he heard the horse.
6. The wicked sailors were choosing spears and swords.
7. The good boy was reading a new book.
8. The boys and the girls sleep in the town.
9. The horse was standing on the earth.
10. Because the girls were frightened, they did not reply.

Exercise 7.4

1. *prīmus nauta hastam habet.*
2. *secundus magister librum portat.*
3. *fēmina proelium timet.*
4. *puella īnsulam spectat.*
5. *puer equum videt.*

6.   *prīmī virī ā secundō templō discēdēbant.*
7.   *quid agricolae nautīs ostendunt?*
8.   *clārus magister decimum librum scrīpsit.*
9.   *pulchra fēmina in viā octāvā habitābat.*
10. *septimōne puerō librum dedistī?*

Exercise 7.5

1.	legible	5.	fortitude
2.	scribe	6.	quarter
3.	regal	7.	octave
4.	servile	8.	decimal

Exercise 7.6

1.   *puella nautam timet.*
2.   *agricola caelum spectat.*
3.   *magister puerum laudat.*
4.   *dominus servum terret.*
5.   *nūntius poētam audit.*
6.   *puella nautās timet; itaque ex templō venit* (or *ex templō igitur venit*).
7.   *veniēbantne ab īnsulā?*
8.   *nūntiōsne audīvistis?*
9.   *quis nautās in oppidum dūcēbat?*
10. *cūr incolae ancillās monēbant?*

Exercise 7.7

1.   (a) To eat food.
     (b) To drink wine.
     (c) To take away gold.
     (d) Marcus, a farmer's son.
     (e) He runs through secret routes (lit. ways).
     (f) They destroy their food.
          They destroy their wine.
          They carry their gold to a secret place.
     (g) *statim* (= immediately).

2.   The sailors hurry to the town and decide to eat food there and to drink wine and to take away gold. But Marcus, a farmer's son, leaves (lit. departs from) the fields and runs by (lit. through) secret routes (lit. ways) into the town. There he shouts "Wicked sailors are hurrying to (lit. into) the town and are seeking our gold." Immediately, the inhabitants, on hearing (lit. when they hear) about the sailors, destroy (their) food and wine and carry (their) gold to (lit. into) a secret place.

3.   (a) Present infinitive
     (b) Present infinitive
     (c) That it is 3rd conjugation
     (d) Genitive
     (e) *ad oppidum* = to the town
          per sēcrētās viās = through secret ways
          in oppidum = into the town
          in locum = into a place (any two of these)

(f) *ab agrīs* = from the fields
      dē nautīs = about the sailors
(g) *dēlēvērunt*
(h) *aurum*

On vēnī, vīdī, vīcī!

Pharnaces II was the son of Mithridates VI (the Great) of Pontus (in Asia Minor). He was favoured by Pompey, and during the war between Pompey and Caesar, he managed to acquire much territory. But he was defeated in 47B.C. by Caesar at Zela, an ancient city in Pontus.

Exercise 7.8

1. Two boys played (or have played) in the street.
2. The poet has written three books.
3. Why did you (s.) run (or have you run) out of the town?
4. The master led (or has led) the slaves into the temple.
5. The queen has reigned (or The queen reigned) for a long time.
6. Have you (s.) eaten food (or Did you eat the food)?
7. I sent (or have sent) a messenger into the town.
8. The farmer departed (or has departed) from (lit. out of) the field.

Exercise 7.9

1. *puella servum monet.*
2. *dominus ancillam vocat.*
3. *fēmina poētam laudat.*
4. *puer agrum spectat.*
5. *nūntiī ab īnsulā discessērunt.*
6. *quid incolīs dīxērunt poētae?*
7. *agricolae quattuor equōs in agrum dūxērunt.*
8. *puerī in oppidō lūsērunt.*

Exercise 7.10

1. *agricola, agricolae,* m. = farmer
2. *fēmina, fēminae,* f. = woman
3. *incola, incolae,* c. = inhabitant
4. *ager, agrī,* m. = field
5. *magister, magistrī,* m. = teacher, master
6. *bellum, bellī,* n. = war
7. *īnsula, īnsulae,* f. = island
8. *vīnum, vīnī,* n. = wine
9. *mūrus, mūrī,* m. = wall
10. *proelium, proeliī,* n. = battle
11. *equus, equī,* m. = horse
12. *īra, īrae,* f. = anger

Exercise 7.11

1. (a) He was very angry about their existence.
    (b) He ordered (his) slaves to throw them into the river (Tiber).
    (c) A she-wolf, a shepherd (Faustulus) and his wife.
    (d) As big and strong.
    (e) That they had many friends.

2. Amulius was very (lit. greatly) angry about Rhea Silvia's sons (lit. because Rhea Silvia had sons); he therefore ordered (his) slaves to throw the twins into the river; the river was the Tiber. A she-wolf saved the little twins there, and she suckled them. Afterwards, a shepherd, Faustulus, carried (them) to his wife; they took care of the twins. At last Romulus and Remus grew (lit. were) big and strong and had many friends. They entered Alba Longa and they said there "We are the sons of Mars and Rhea Silvia; we are Romulus and Remus.

3.   (a) *habeō, habēre, habuī, habitum* = I have
    (b) *iubeō, iubēre, iussī, iussum* = I order
    (c) *parvōs gemellōs* = little twins
        multōs amīcōs = many friends
        Rōmulus et Remus: magnī et validī (the adjectives here are complements)
    (d) *dīcō, dīcere, dīxī, dictum* = I say
    (e) *erāmus*

Chapter 8

On adverbs

Due to the absence in the Level 1 syllabus of any regular adverbs from adjectives in '-*us*', teachers will have to choose when is the best time to teach the regular formation of such adverbs. A simple explanation may suffice at this stage:

For adverbs formed from adjectives in -*us*, replace -*us* with -*ē*.

E.g. *clārē* = clearly, from *clārus* = clear.

For adverbs formed from adjectives in -*er*, add -*ē* to the stem.

E.g. *miserē* = wretchedly from *miser* = wretched.

E.g. *pulchrē* = beautifully from *pulcher* = beautiful.

Adverbs may indeed be weak parts of speech compared with verbs and nouns. But I think the Romans had a very soft spot for them. Trust Terence to have cashed in on this in the *Phormio* again, when the pompous Demipho addresses his three friends at the beginning of Act II with the lines:

> *ēnumquam quoiquam contumēliōsius*
> *audīstis factam iniūriam quam haec est mihi?'*

How Terence must have revelled in *'ēnumquam'* and *'contumēliōsius'* in his adoptive language!

In *Aeneid* v, 389, Acestes brings out the poignancy of Entellus' age by addressing the old hero thus:

> *'Entelle, hērōum quondam fortissime frūstrā.'*

My favourite piece with adverbs comes in Petronius, *Satyricon* 45. Echion, in proverbial mood, when commenting on life, says:

> *'modo sīc, modo sīc',* ait rūsticus, varium porcum perdiderat.*
> 'One minute thus, one minute thus,' (as) the countryman said (when) he had lost his spotted pig!

Why did the *'rūsticus'* say *'modo sīc, modo sīc'*? Was he making a philosophical comment on the loss of his spotted pig? This seems extremely unlikely. And why was the pig spotted? Does this add anything to the sad tale? I think it does. The poor old *'rūsticus'* had (note the tense) lost his pig. When asked to describe it, he would not have known a sophisticated adjective like *varius* (Greek ποικίλος); but he knew his adverbs – 'now thus, now thus' (i.e. 'a bit like this, a bit like that', no doubt accompanied by manual gestures); in other words, 'spotted'.

Exercise 8.1

1. Slaves sing when they are building (lit. making) a wall.
2. What did the sailors take (or have the sailors taken) out of the town?
3. The sailors wish to shoot (lit. throw) arrows into the town.
4. The wind made (or has made) many waves.
5. We were throwing spears into the wall.
6. Do you (pl.) wish to read a book?
7. Why do you (s.) not wish to prepare food in the town?
8. I wish to take gold and money.

Exercise 8.2

1. *fēmina cibum parat.*
2. *puer poētam laudat.*
3. *magistrī fīlius agrum videt.*
4. *nauta gladium portat.*
5. *quid ab īnsulā capiēbant?*
6. *scūta in locōs altōs iaciēbāmus.*
7. *quid faciunt nūntiī in templō?*
8. *parvae puellae per agrōs currere cupiēbant.*

Exercise 8.3

1. (a) Near the town.
    (b) Their wish to eat and drink.
    (c) It means "in the town" (lit. there).
    (d) No.
    (e) Digging (lit. they move earth).
    (f) Because they had nothing to eat or drink.
    (g) Because they found no gold.
    (h) They decided to depart from the town and from the island.
    (i) Because they had fooled and foiled the sailors and are safe.

N.B. The suggested answers for (f) and (g) are interchangeable!

2. When the sailors were near the city, they greatly desired to eat and drink. Soon they ran into the city; however, there was not (any) food there, (and) there was not (any) wine. They summoned (lit. called) the inhabitants; there were also not (any) inhabitants there. They wished to take gold out of the earth; they dug (lit. move) the earth; there was (lit. is) not (any) gold there. At last, the sailors, miserable and angry, decided to depart from (lit. out of) the town and from the island. The inhabitants watched and laughed and sang (out) "We are happy because we are safe."

3. (a) Where?
    (b) Present infinitives
    (c) *capere* = to take (line 4)
        discēdere = to depart (line 6)
    (d) Accusative: *vocant*
    (e) Accusative
    (f) Nominative
    (g) Nominative: *nautae*

Exercise 8.4

1. Quintus warned (or has warned) the inhabitants about the danger.
2. The women had (or have had) much gold.
3. Have you (s) held (or did you hold) a sword and a spear?
4. When the teacher came, the boys were sleeping.
5. Aulus did not fear the horse.

6.   Why did you (pl.) terrify (or have you terrified) the horses?
7.   What were you (pl.) hearing about the farmers?
8.   The teachers used to come into the temple with the boys.
9.   We were hearing the words of the poet.
10.   We have heard the words of the poet.

Exercise 8.5

1.   *dominus servum terret.*
2.   *puella magistrum timet.*
3.   *saevus nauta hastam tenet.*
4.   *ancilla cibum parat.*
5.   *puer scūtum portat.*
6.   *agricolae incolās dē nautīs monuērunt.*
7   *puellae poētās audiēbant.*
8.   *puerī, ubi vēnērunt, magistrum audīvērunt.*
9.   *equī in agrō dormiēbant.*
10.   *incolae multum aurum habēbant.*

Exercise 8.6

1.   Hear the words of the teacher.
2.   Build three walls in the field.
3.   Friend, take four books into the town.
4.   Lead the little boys into the temple.
5   Slave, stay in the town.
6.   Teachers, depart from the fields.
7.   Boys, come into the town.
8.   Warn the farmers about the sailors.
9.   Girls, reply to the women.
10.   Maid-servants, prepare food.

Exercise 8.7

1.   *magister puerōs monet.*
2.   *nauta gladium tenet.*
3.   *puella poētam spectat.*
4.   *puer ancillam vocat.*
5.   *Mārce, equōs in agrum dūc.*
6.   *puerī, librōs in templum capite.*
7   *Aule, ā pulchrā īnsulā discēde.*
8.   *Sexte, in agrō cum parvīs puellīs ambulā.*
9.   *Cassia, cibum prope oppidum cōnsūme.*
10.   *agricolae, saevōs virōs ex agrīs currere iubēte.*

Exercise 8.8

I must admit that I find it incredibly hard to stomach the casual way in which Romulus' murder of Remus is generally mentioned. I can see that it must have been infuriating for Romulus after all his effort building those walls to see them contemptuously leapt over. But one would have thought that at least some sort of curse should have been imprecated upon Romulus and his city after the perpetration of such a cruel and senseless murder of the brother who had shared all his hardship and success. Instead, we are told that Romulus reigned 37 years, was ultimately taken up to heaven and was worshipped on earth. Robert Graves suggests that the murder may have been the result of a widespread custom of sacrificing a royal prince at the foundation of a city, and he quotes 1 Kings, 16, 34. I find this pretty unconvincing. In the immortal words of Gomme (A.W. Gomme, Historical Commentary on Thucydides, Vol. 1, O.U.P., 1945, p. 401), at the end of page after page of exhaustive (and exhausting) quotations delving into the chronology of Themistocles' flight to Asia Minor in Thucydides Book 1 – 'the question remains unsolved.'

I feel rather bad about calling Rome an *'oppidum'.* But *urbs,* alas, is 3rd declension.

1.   (a) He was terrified of (lit. feared greatly) Romulus and Remus.
    (b) The fact that Romulus and Remus killed him.
    (c) To found a new town.
    (d) He was looking at the walls.
    (e) Happy.
    (f) He jumped over the walls.
    (g) It made him feel angry, and he killed Remus.

2.   Amulius was terrified of (lit. feared greatly) Romulus and Remus, when they entered Alba Longa; Romulus and Remus killed Amulius. Numitor was king of (lit. ruled) Alba Longa again; the twins decided to found a new town; this (lit. the) town was Rome. Romulus built the walls and was looking at them happily (lit. happy); Remus, however, jumped over the walls; Romulus, angry at Remus' having jumped over (lit. because Remus jumped over) the walls of Rome, killed Remus.

3.   (a) *timeō, timēre, timuī,* no supine = I fear
    (b) *regō, regere, rēxī, rēctum* = I rule
    (c) Accusative
    (d) Nominative
    (e) *Rōmulus*

Exercise 8.9

1.   near = *prope* + acc.
2.   against = *contrā* + acc.
3.   to = *ad* + acc.
4.   into = *in* + acc.
5.   out of = *ex* + abl.
6.   across = *trāns* + acc.
7.   through = *per* + acc.
8.   in = *in* + abl.

Exercise 8.10

(a) prime
(b) multitude
(c) clear
(d) altitude
(e) peril

Exercise 8.11

1. The boys were absent from the temple.
2. The farmers are often absent from the fields.
3. We always wish to be absent from a battle.
4. Why were you (s.) absent from the town?
5. The messengers were (or have been) absent from the place.
6. The good women decided (or have decided) to be present at the temple.
7. Who is present there now?
8. The sailor's daughter was present at the road.
9. Therefore we were (or have been) present at the wall.
10. Slave, come to me.

Exercise 8.12

1. *Aulus mūrum aedificat.*
2. *ancilla cibum parat.*
3. *nauta scūtum tenet.*
4. *Mārcus agrum intrat.*
5. *poēta librum portat.*
6. *ab oppidō absumus.*
7. *puerī, quod nōn aderant, aberant.*
8. *ancillae ab īnsulā numquam absunt.*
9. *sociī adfuērunt.*
10. *bonae puellae semper adsunt.*

Exercise 8.13

1. (a) Once upon a time.
   (b) *ōlim.*
   (c) Because they did not wish to overcome the inhabitants.
   (d) Much food and water.
   (e) A big book.
   (f) Quintus, the poet.
   (g) Beautiful words.
   (h) It was easy when the winds were favourable (lit. good), but dangerous when they were unfavourable (lit. bad).

2. Once upon a time, five boys with five girls, decided to seek a new island. They did not wish to overcome the inhabitants there, but to find gold. They did not take swords and spears across the waves, but a great deal of food and a great deal of water and a large book. Quintus, the poet, wrote the book and gave it to the little sailors; it was beautiful and contained beautiful words; the

sailors greatly loved the book. They sailed bravely through the waves; when the winds were favourable (lit. good), they were happy, but when they were unfavourable (lit. bad) they were unhappy because they were in great danger. At last, they found an island; they hurry into the town. There, the inhabitants bid welcome (lit. say "be of good cheer") to the sailors.

3. (a) Present infinitive.
    (b) Yes: *superāre* (line 2), *invenīre* (line 3).
    (c) 3rd conjugation.
    (d) *liber* (understood).
    (e) Accusative.
    (f) *fortiter* (they were sailing bravely).
    (g) *ventus bonus fuit.*
    (h) *quod in magnō perīculō erant.*

Chapter 9

On subordinate clauses and word order (the Chinese puzzle)

A friend of mine used to create what I think he called Chinese puzzles. This involved fitting lots of wooden pieces into each other, such that, until just before the very end, you could demolish the whole structure with the flick of a finger; and then he put the last bit in and, lo, you could throw it against a wall, trample on it, or assail it with a hammer and it would remain a solid, immutable unit. So it is with many a Latin sentence, where everything remains, as it were, embryonic, until you bring in the last word; and then it is inseparably bound together, an organic whole.

Exercise 9.1

1. *Rōmulus, ubi Remus mūrōs spectāvit, īrātus erat.*
   When Remus looked at the walls, Romulus was angry.

2. *Rōmulus, quod Remus mūrōs spectāvit, īrātus erat.*
   Because Remus looked at the walls, Romulus was angry.

3. *Amūlius Rōmulum, ubi Albam Longam intrāvit, magnopere timuit.*
   Amulius feared Romulus greatly, when he entered Alba Longa.

4. *nautae, ubi prope oppidum stant, vīnum bibere cupiunt.*
   When they stand near the town, the sailors wish to drink wine.

5. *Amūlius, quod Rhēa Silvia fīliōs habuit, īrātus erat.*
   Because Rhea Silvia had sons, Amulius was angry.

Exercise 9.2

I cannot claim that this is an exhaustive account of the 2nd Punic War. To get a slightly more informative version of the crossing of the Alps, I suggest a dip into Livy Book 21.

1. (a) The fact that he often used to hear (the words) "The Romans are wicked; they wish to destroy us and our town" again and again.
   (b) He was a boy.
   (c) When he was a man.
   (d) He decided to make his way (lit. depart) across the Alps (lit. high Alpine places) into Italy.
   (e) Many Carthaginians and many allies.
   (f) He also took (some) elephants, because he wished to terrify the Romans.
   (g) Not really; it is redundant. It has been amply implied already.

2. Hannibal was a Carthaginian; when he was a boy he often used to hear (spoken) again and again (the words) "The Romans are wicked; they wish to destroy us and our town." He was in Spain for (lit. through) many years and when he was a man, he often used to say "I wish to destroy Rome". And so he decided to make his way (lit. depart) across the Alps (lit. high Alpine places) into Italy. Therefore he took (lit. led) many Carthaginians and many allies (with him) and set out (lit. departed). He also took (lit. led) many elephants because he wished to terrify the Romans. Hannibal did not like the Romans!

3.   (a) Nominative.
      (b) Subordinate.
      (c) Nominative.
      (d) *cupere.*
      (e) Nominative.
      (f) It is the present infinitive of *discēdō.*
      (g) It is a subordinate clause. It does not come at the end of the sentence, this position being regularly reserved for the main verb.

Exercise 9.3

1.   He, she or it used to overcome.
2.   He, she or it terrified.
3.   We were making (or doing).
4.   They warned (have warned).
5.   He, she asked, asked for (has asked, has asked for).
6.   You (pl.) have taken (took).
7.   You (s.) have slept (you slept).
8.   They are coming.
9.   He, she or it remained (has remained).
10.   We ran (have run).

Exercise 9.4

1.   *prope rēgīnam*
2.   *in agrō*
3.   *cum puerō*
4.   *dē proeliō*
5.   *ex oppidō*
6.   *in īnsulam*
7.   *ā templō*
8.   *dē mūrīs*
9.   *per viam*
10. *trāns undās*

Exercise 9.5

1.   (a) They placed (their) book on a table and decided to read.
      (b) They asked "What are you doing?"
      (c) They did not know what a book was.
      (d) They showed them words.
      (e) Because the inhabitants did not understand.
      (f) They suddenly sang (the words).
      (g) *laetī* (happy)
      (h) (To be able) to read.
      (i) They asked the sailors to teach them (lit. teach us).

2.   When they had eaten (some) food and drunk (some) water, the sailors placed (their) book on a table and decided to read. "What are you doing?" asked the inhabitants. The sailors replied "We are reading a book." "What is a book?" they (the inhabitants) asked again. The sailors did not reply. "What is there in a book?" "There are words in a book". The sailors showed the words to the inhabitants. However, the inhabitants did not understand. Suddenly, the sailors sang (the words). The inhabitants, happy now, were singing with the sailors. They said "We also wish to read. Teach us."

3. (a) *pōnō, pōnere, posuī, positum* = I place, put.
    (b) Present infinitive.
    (c) Nominative.
    (d) Accusative.
    (e) Dative.
    (f) Ablative.
    (g) It is governed by *'cum'*.
    (h) In line 8 it is nominative; in line 9 it is accusative.
    (i) It is the imperative (2nd person plural).

Exercise 9.6

1. *laetōrum poētārum*
2. *miserī puerī*
3. *fessīs fēminīs*
4. *cum multīs puellīs*
5. *ō laete domine*
6. *ex magnō oppidō*
7. *trāns altās undās*
8. *per pulchrōs agrōs*
9. *saevum proelium*
10. *saevum proelium*

Exercise 9.7

¹e	g	²o		³c	u	⁴r
g		⁵d	e	a		e
o		o		n		p
	⁶a	m	o	t	e	
⁷d		i		a		⁸m
u		⁹n	o	n		e
¹⁰o	g	e		¹¹t	u	a

Exercise 9.8

1. (a) They taught them to read.
    (b) They wished to sail (back) to (their) fatherland. However, they did not wish to depart from the inhabitants.
    (c) Presumably because they did not want the sailors to depart.
    (d) Yes.
    (e) No.
    (f) To come (back) again to their new friends.
    (g) Return.

2.   The sailors slept in the town and stayed there for a long time; they taught the inhabitants to read. But at last, they wished to sail (back) to (lit. into) (their) fatherland. However, they did not wish to depart from the inhabitants. Both the inhabitants and the sailors were unhappy; but at last the sailors were departing and they said to the inhabitants "We have found not gold but friends. Therefore we are happy." And the inhabitants said "Come again to your new friends; you also are our friends." And when they were already sailing, the sailors cried out (lit. shouted) "Farewell," and the inhabitants cried "Farewell."

3.   (a) Present infinitive.
     (b) *legere* (line 2), *discēdere* (line 3).
     (c) *in oppidō* = in the town.
         in patriam = to (lit. into) (their) fatherland.
         ab incolīs = from the inhabitants.
         ad vestrōs novōs amīcōs = to your new friends.
     (d) Accusative.
     (e) *tamen* = however (line 3); *igitur* = therefore (line 6).
     (f) *venīte* = come (2nd person plural).
     (g) By putting the noun (*amīcōs*) at the end of the sentence instead of the verb, we are stressing it.

Exercise 9.9

1.   *quis hīc habitat?*
2.   *Aule, cūr vēnistī?*
3.   *agricolae servus subitō in templum cucurrit.*
4.   *audiuntne puerī magistrum?*
5.   *pugnābantne fortiter nautae?*
6.   *fuitne pulcher liber in templō?*
7.   *cūr statim oppidum intrāvērunt?*
8.   *quid legit?*
9.   *ubi est īnsulae rēgīna?*
10. *Rōmānī patriam (suam) magnopere amant.*

Chapter 10

On 'nunc est bibendum'

I like to imagine that Horace often thought of a 'famous bit' like this and scribbled it down and kept it under his pillow until something 'famous' happened like the defeat of Antony and Cleopatra.

In a similar vein, we have slightly changed this and applied it to the great fact that we have now reached our last chapter.

On stories etc.

In this chapter we have set three stories modelled literally on the Common Entrance exam: with a little piece from English into Latin again strictly in accord with the syllabus.

Hints on doing exams

I'm sure we all have our special 'things' to hold forth about on this great subject. For what it's worth, here are a few of my 'things' as I have delivered them to the victims-to-be, before they proceed to translate Latin into English.

1. Procure a coil of sturdy cord; take it into the exam-room with you, and arrange for your hands to be bound tightly behind your chair. If this is impossible, the next best thing is to clasp your hands together behind you.
2. Read the English at the top of the passage, and look for any words, the English of which they may give you. You'd be surprised how many people forget to do this.
3. Read the passage through quickly, to break the ice, i.e. to get a general idea what it's about.
4. Read the passage slowly; in each sentence or clause look for the main verb first and then for the subject in the nominative case, which is almost certainly lurking around.
5. There is almost certain to be a bit or two which does not yield immediately to treatment. Attack these bits viciously like a dog at a bone. You've forgotten the meaning of a word; perhaps an English word it reminds you of will help; in the last resort, guess, but guess intelligently: in other words use all the words round it to help, and whatever you end up with, make sure that you have translated the case or the gender or the person of the unknown word correctly. Consider: *pulchrōs equōs amat.* You've forgotten the meaning of *pulchrōs*. English words won't help. Well at least in your translation make sure that *pulchrōs* agrees with *equōs* . And then, all things being equal, what sort of horses is he likely to love? All this will help to get it right or at least only slightly wrong.
6. Above all, DON'T feel that you simply must cover the piece of paper in front of you as quickly as possible. One correct sentence will earn you more marks than a whole incorrect page. And DON'T try to make 'sense' of the passage by abandoning what you know and translating any of it by something you really know to be wrong.
7. When you have done (and not done!) all this, then and then only should your hands be released!
8. I'm afraid you do have to keep an eye on the clock too.

Exercise 10.1

Atalanta strikes me as a thoroughly nasty piece of work. And I'm not greatly enamoured of Hippomenes either. So I'm not terribly sorry about their end. According to Ovid, Venus (Greek Aphrodite) made them offend Cybele (the Great Mother), who turned them into lions and got them to flank her throne. They were also unable to pursue their mutual relationship. Whether this was a curse or a blessing is a moot point! According to some sources Atalanta's husband was not Hippomenes but Milanion.

(a) That she ought not to marry (lit. to have a husband).
(b) Because she was beautiful and bright.
(c) She raced (lit. ran against) them.
(d) He would be the only one she desired to marry (see translation below).
(e) She would kill them.
(f) With a spear.
(g) Many men were prepared to risk their lives racing her. She always won!
(h) By standing at the end of the sentence, where the verb would normally stand, ´nēmō´ is strongly stressed.

Translation of the passage (not required of pupil):
(Once upon a time, the god terrified the girl Atalanta saying (lit. who said) "You ought not to have a husband." Atalanta was beautiful and bright; and many men greatly desired to marry Atalanta. And so the girl used to race (lit. run against) the men who wished to marry her (lit. Atalanta). And because she feared having (lit. to have) a husband, she used to say "I wish to have no husband except the man who beats me (in the race). And I have decided to kill with a spear the men who do not beat me (in the race.)" Many men raced (lit. ran against) the girl. However, no one at all beat her (the girl).)

Exercise 10.2

Many men raced (lit. ran against) Atalanta, and the girl killed many with a spear. But the boy Hippomenes, who was in Atalanta's fatherland, saw the men who raced (lit. ran against) Atalanta, and he laughed and said "The men who raced (lit. ran against) the girl were stupid. She has already killed many with a spear. Me however she has not killed. But suddenly he saw the girl and immediately loved her and wished to marry her.

Exercise 10.3

(a) Dative.
(b) Third person singular, perfect; *currō.*
(c) *contrā puellam* = against the girl.
    ad terram = to the earth.
(d) *superābat* (imperfect) in line 2 means she kept beating (lit. overcoming, i.e. being ahead of) him, but *superāvit* (past) in line 4 means that the boy beat (lit. overcame) her in the end.
(e) *capiō, capere, cēpī, captum* = I take; capture.
(f) *capiēbat.*
(g) *puer; puerum.*
(h) *dea.*

Tranlsation of the passage (not required of pupil):
The goddess Venus gave three golden apples to the boy. Hippomenes raced (lit. ran against) the girl bravely, but the girl kept beating (lit. overcoming) (him); therefore the boy threw an apple to the ground three times, and three times the girl stopped (lit. stood) and picked up (lit. took) the apple; in this way (lit. thus) the boy at last beat (lit. overcame) the girl. The girl now loved the boy; they were happy. But the goddess punished the boy and the girl because they were not grateful.

Exercise 10.4

(a) *cibum parāmus*

(b) *fēmina ancillam videt*

Exercise 10.5

(a) That he was king of (lit. ruled) the gods.
(b) Angry........<u>with</u> Phoebus.
(c) To be a slave on earth for (lit. through) one year.
(d) You must be.
(e) He asked the inhabitants "Where am I?"
(f) He asked "Who is your king?" (lit. rules you?)
(g) He told them to lead him to Admetus.
   (This is in line 7; with apologies.)
(h) A palace (in line 7, with apologies again).

Translation of the passage (not required of pupil):
Jupiter was king of (lit. ruled) the gods. Phoebus Apollo was a great god; once upon a time Jupiter was very angry with Phoebus and said to the god "You must be a slave on earth for (lit. through) one year, and he threw Phoebus down from the sky to earth. There he asked the inhabitants "Where am I?" The inhabitants answered "You are in Greece, in Thessaly." He asked again "Who is your king?" (lit. rules you). They replied "Admetus is our king" (lit. rules us.): "Lead me to Admetus," said Apollo.

N.B. Apollo had killed the Cyclopes, who used to make Jupiter's thunderbolts.

Exercise 10.6

This story is best known from the beautiful handling of it by Euripides, the last of the three great Athenian tragedians (485?-406BC?). His *Alcestis*, though it ends happily, is full of human suffering, sympathy and even humour. A strange feature of the story is that it seems in order for Admetus to expect someone to die instead of him. He is certainly overcome with grief at his wife's death.

Hercules was a great friend of Admetus', and could not understand why he and his friends were not received cheerfully and enthusiastically on this occasion. As a model of politeness Admetus did not want his servants to tell Hercules about Alcestis' death. But this was asking too much of one of them, a faithful old retainer.

For Hercules this was nothing! The play ends in great happiness. I certainly think one's pupils would enjoy reading a good modern translation of it.

Admetus was a good man; he never made Phoebus miserable. At last the god was departing to the sky, and he said to Admetus "Because you were a good master, when you have to depart to the Underworld, if another (person) wishes to depart instead of you, you (yourself) need not depart." When Admetus had to depart to the Underworld, he asked many (people is understood). However, they did not wish to depart instead of Admetus. But at last Alcestis decided to depart instead of her husband.

Exercise 10.7

(a) *vīsit*
(b) *miserum*
(c) *cantāvērunt; clāmāvērunt*
(d) *cum amīcīs* = with friends
   cum Lētō = with Death
   cum fēminā = with a woman
   ad Admētum = to Admetus
(e) *miserae*
(f) feminine
(g) *videō, vidēre, vīdī, vīsum* = I see; *videt*

Translation of the passage (not required of pupil):
(Suddenly Hercules with his friends, visited Admetus (who was) unhappy because of his wife's
death (lit. because his wife had departed); they kept singing and shouting, and Hercules asked a
slave "Why are you (pl.) miserable?" The slave answered "Because Alcestis is dead."
Immediately Hercules himself fought with Death. Hercules overcame Death and came to
Admetus with a woman. When Admetus saw the woman, he cried out (lit. shouted) "It is
Alcestis" and he was happy.)

Exercise 10.8

(i) *agricola mūrum aedificat.*
(ii) *rēgīna puellam terret.*

Exercise 10.9

(a) King of Athens; king of Crete.
(b) Son of Aegeus.
(c) An island.
(d) As both a man and a bull.
(e) Minos had been conducting (lit. making) a savage war against Athens for a long time (line 4).
(f) They had to send seven boys and seven girls to Crete, to the Minotaur (lines 5-6).
(g) Across the waves (line 5).

Translation of the passage (not required of pupil):
Aegeus was king of (lit. ruled) Athens. He had a son. The son was Theseus. Minos was king of
(lit. ruled) the island Crete; Minos also had a son, the Minotaur, who was both a man and a bull.
Minos was conducting a savage war against Athens for a long time; and the inhabitants of Athens
had to send seven boys and seven girls across the waves to Crete, to the Minotaur.

N.B. Different versions of the story exist, particularly with regard to the frequency with which the
Athenians were obliged to send the boys and girls.

Exercise 10.10

There is a lot of sadness in this story again, and there was a lot more in store for Theseus often brought by him on to himself. Perhaps he is a good example of the Greek belief that the more successful you were, the more you had to fear that the gods, out of jealousy, would take you down many a peg. It was even dangerous to be greatly loved by a particular god or goddess lest this brought you into disfavour with another god or goddess who was on bad terms with the god or goddess who loved you.

Theseus decided to sail to Crete with the boys and girls. Minos had a daughter; (this) daughter was Ariadne; when the boys and girls arrived in (lit. came to) Crete, Ariadne saw the prince and fell in love with (lit. loved) (him) and gave him (lit. to the prince) a thread. Slaves took (lit. led) the boys and girls to the Minotaur, who lived in a labyrinth. There, seven girls and six boys were wretched and terrified. The seventh boy, however, Theseus, was not afraid (lit. did not fear), but he killed the Minotaur and with the help of the thread made his way (lit. departed) out of the labyrinth.

Exercise 10.11

(a) *laetus* = happy; *ingrātus* = ungrateful
(b) *nāvigāvit*
(c) *relīquērunt*
(d) *cum amīcīs* = with (his) friends
   cum Ariadnā = with Ariadne
   ad patriam = to (his) fatherland
   in Naxō = in Naxus (This island is generally known by its Greek name, Naxos.)
   in patriam = into (his) fatherland
   ex perīculō = out of danger
(e) *Ariadnam*
(f) Patriotic
(g) *magnīs perīculīs*
(h) *suīs, laeta, ingrata, magnā, tuta, misera*
(i) The ship that sailed to Crete had black sails, but Theseus had arranged with his father that, if he returned successful, he would hoist a white sail. This he forgot to do, and when Aegeus saw that no such sail had been hoisted, he assumed his son was dead and either fell or threw himself into the sea, to his own death. The sea, the Aegean is said to be named after him.

Translation of the passage (not required of pupil):
Theseus was sailing happily (lit. happy) with his friends and with Ariadne to his fatherland. But he was ungrateful, and he left Ariadne in Naxos, an island. There, the god Bacchus saw Ariadne and loved her and married her. But when Theseus arrived in (lit. came into) his fatherland having safely escaped from (lit. safe out of) great danger, he was immediately unhappy.

Exercise 10.12

(i) *rēgīna librum tenet.*
(ii) *equus poētam spectat.*